To my daughter Carys and my son Jem, who have provided much inspiration and many welcome interruptions while I was writing this book.

Contents

KT-572-050

Meet the author

As someone who is fortunate enough to earn a living through writing, I've always been fascinated by the creative process. But it wasn't until I became a parent that I realized how incredibly creative we all are as children, and how slowly, as we grow, we begin to lose that natural curiosity, playfulness and freedom of thought which enables us to look at the world in an entirely new way every day.

We don't have to lose these abilities. I hope to give you some insights and ideas as to how you can help your child to develop their own unique imaginations and creative talents. When you do, you will be giving your child a gift which will enhance their lives in so many different ways. What you'll also find is that, in order to encourage your child's creativity, you'll need to be imaginative and open to all kinds of new (and silly, and messy) experiences yourself.

I hope you and your children enjoy yourselves as much as my children, their Dad and I did while we were trying out the ideas ourselves.

Victoria Wilson, 2010

Image credits

Front cover: © Michael Hitoshi/Digital Vision/Getty Images

Back cover: © Jakub Semeniuk/iStockphoto.com, © Royalty-Free/Corbis, © agencyby/iStockphoto.com, © Andy Cook/iStockphoto.com, © Christopher Ewing/iStockphoto.com, © zebicho – Fotolia.com, © Geoffrey Holman/iStockphoto.com, © Photodisc/Getty Images, © James C. Pruitt/iStockphoto.com, © Mohamed Saber – Fotolia.com

Only got a minute?

All children are naturally creative, but studies reveal that it's possible to increase creative 'IQ', particularly in young children. Here are a few things you can try right now to boost your child's curiosity and imagination.

First of all, make a space in your home where your child can sit to read, draw or make things. This space, while safely supervised, should be away from the prying eyes of anyone who happens to pop into the house, and where your child doesn't feel 'watched'. Putting a box of books and paper and pens in the corner of the living room, or even giving them their own spot at a table or on a kitchen counter can be enough. If they feel safe and they feel the area is 'theirs' you'll find they settle there more happily, and then the magic can start.

Make some food pictures. Use raw peppers, spaghetti, baked beans on toast – anything you like. This has the advantage of being something you can build around mealtimes so it doesn't take up precious time,

Boost Your Child's Creativity
Victoria Wilson

For UK order enquiries: please contact Bookpoint Ltd, 130 Milton Park, Abingdon, Oxon OX14 4SB. Telephone: +44 (0) 1235 827720. Fax: +44 (0) 1235 400454. Lines are open 09.00–17.00, Monday to Saturday, with a 24-hour message answering service. Details about our titles and how to order are available at www.teachyourself.com

For USA order enquiries: please contact McGraw-Hill Customer Services, PO Box 545, Blacklick, OH 43004-0545, USA. Telephone: 1-800-722-4726. Fax: 1-614-755-5645.

For Canada order enquiries: please contact McGraw-Hill Ryerson Ltd, 300 Water St, Whitby, Ontario L1N 9B6, Canada. Telephone: 905 430 5000. Fax: 905 430 5020.

Long renowned as the authoritative source for self-guided learning – with more than 50 million copies sold worldwide – the *Teach Yourself* series includes over 500 titles in the fields of languages, crafts, hobbies, business, computing and education.

British Library Cataloguing in Publication Data: a catalogue record for this title is available from the British Library.

Library of Congress Catalog Card Number: on file.

First published in UK 2009 by Hodder Education, part of Hachette UK, 338 Euston Road, London NW1 3BH.

First published in US 2009 by The McGraw-Hill Companies, Inc.

This edition published 2010.

Previously published as *Teach Yourself Developing Your Child's Creativity*

The *Teach Yourself* name is a registered trade mark of Hodder Headline.

Typeset by MPS Limited, a Macmillan Company.

Printed in Great Britain for Hodder Education, an Hachette UK Company, 338 Euston Road, London NW1 3BH, by CPI Cox & Wyman, Reading, Berkshire RG1 8EX.

The publisher has used its best endeavours to ensure that the URLs for external websites referred to in this book are correct and active at the time of going to press. However, the publisher and the author have no responsibility for the websites and can make no guarantee that a site will remain live or that the content will remain relevant, decent or appropriate.

Hachette UK's policy is to use papers that are natural, renewable and recyclable products and made from wood grown in sustainable forests. The logging and manufacturing processes are expected to conform to the environmental regulations of the country of origin.

Impression number	10 9 8 7 6 5 4 3 2 1
Year	2014 2013 2012 2011 2010

and you're also breaking some rules (don't play with your food). Occasionally breaking minor rules is a good way to encourage your child to be a bit more imaginative and to be more daring when coming up with new ideas.

Get your children to create a sun or rain dance. You'll bring music and fun into the house, and also get them to combine concepts (weather and music) that don't necessarily go together, helping to inspire imagination.

Dress up as a character for tea. Get the whole family involved. You can't expect to inspire creativity if you don't act as a good role model and join in.

Finally, make a point of noticing the less obvious ways your child is creative (often this is when they are being very naughty). Do they find unusual ways to get into the biscuit tin? Do they bend the truth slightly to make a story more interesting? Obviously, don't encourage bad behaviour, but when you can, point out to them when they've done something creative and praise the ingenuity.

5 Only got five minutes?

There are hundreds of games, activities and things to do, tailored to your child's age and interests, which are designed to encourage them to think more freely and imaginatively. Here are a few you can try to start with.

First, make sure you have somewhere to play music your child loves. For example, set up a stereo in the living room or their bedroom (you can probably get one for free at www.freecycle.com, plus some music to go with it). Make sure there's a little bit of room to dance near the stereo.

Then paint a song. Give your child some paper and crayons or paints and ask them what colours they think go with the song, or what feelings and things the song makes them think about. Get them to put it down on paper. Mixing up ideas like this, imagining sounds as colours, shapes and ideas, really helps to fire imagination and break down barriers to creativity.

Start a scrapbook and/or scrapbox. Make it a tradition to give your child a new one every birthday, Christmas or New Year. Children love to collect things, whether it's leaves or stones from the park, or tickets to the zoo. Help them to write a little story, draw a picture, or stick in photographs or postcards after a big day. It will help them to reinforce memories and it will be their own creative project too.

Have car sing-a-longs – to music they like or to the radio – but fill in silly words in the chorus. Making singing funny, and hearing you singing, makes children less self-conscious about singing and music. They'll be so interested in getting you to sing the right word, or thinking up a funnier (ruder) one of their own, that they'll forget anyone's listening to them sing.

If you haven't already got one, make a dressing-up box. Properly made costumes are actually less fun for children than mum's old oversized shoes and scarves and cardboard swords as they're less adaptable to different games. Find old beads and hats to put in the box. If you have a box already, a short, fun game (which helps you clear out old junk) is to go around the house to top it up.

When you have to do chores, getting your child to copy you is a good way to get them to role-play and have some fun, while getting on with things. While you're vacuuming, for example, get your child to copy, or vacuum their own little area, or playhouse, or give them some cloths and sponges to spruce up their pretend rocket or café, while you're cleaning the kitchen or the car.

Another five-minute task which can encourage creativity is to clear a shelf or some wall space to display particularly special stories, pictures, or things your child has collected or found. Choose things which your child has put a lot of time or thought into, rather than selecting things you yourself think are 'good' or 'pretty', as it is a way or rewarding effort, without being judgmental about the results of those efforts, and this will encourage your child to try new things and to enjoy what they are doing without the fear that it won't turn out perfectly.

Finally, check your child's schedule. Ensure they have enough quiet time and a space they feel safe and secure in, where they can do creative things they dream up by themselves. Sometimes, the best thing you can do to nurture creativity is to give your child the time, space and security to do their own thing.

Introduction

Most parents are well aware that nurturing creativity in children is a 'good thing', without really understanding why this is the case.

To put it simply, encouraging creativity helps your child develop a range of cognitive and life skills which will help them throughout their lives, regardless of which career or lifestyle they choose to follow.

Well-established research reveals that fostering children's creativity from very early on can help them to achieve greater academic and professional success in later life. For example, one study at Yale University revealed that the measure of a young child's creative abilities was more accurate in predicting exam success as they left school than a simple measure of their IQ. Drs Dorothy and Jerome Singer of the Yale Child Study Centre have also carried out several studies which reveal that young children who indulge in imaginative and creative play go on to become more successful in terms of expanding their vocabulary and in tests measuring mathematical abilities and other cognitive skills, than children who are less engaged in these activities.

What these psychologists and others have also discovered is that a child's early life – particularly the first seven years – is the most effective period in which parents and teachers can cultivate a child's creative potential.

As a starting point to fostering the creative abilities which every child possesses, parents and carers need to use their own imaginations to broaden their understanding of what creativity actually is.

All too often we automatically think of 'creative activities' as getting out paint pots, sticking down pictures or making models from empty egg cartons. Perhaps we might sometimes extend that to reading or musical activities.

But by limiting our concept of childhood creativity to the tried and trusted methods of painting, stories and crafts, ironically we are falling into the trap of being very unimaginative ourselves; and it's a limitation which can alter the course of our children's lives.

In this book, the aim is to reveal to you hundreds of different ways in which you can stimulate your child's imagination and encourage them to think in new, exciting and individual ways. Included are ideas to make your home a more creative environment, alterations in the daily routine, as well as a host of games and activities tailored to children of different ages, from newborn to six years old.

As well as giving a basic understanding of the latest studies into children's creativity, the book will also provide basic golden rules to fostering creativity, unravel the false myths we often believe about creative 'types', as well as identifying the common habits that can kill creative potential.

You will also learn why creativity can help your child to develop greater social skills and why it builds academic success.

Moreover, the book will examine whether it is true that some children are simply more creative than others, and how psychologists measure creativity in children.

Perhaps the most important message in this book, however, is to convey just how dramatically you can alter your child's life and future by adopting some of these ideas. Whether your child is the kind of logical and ordered child who lines up toys neatly on shelves or a free spirit who paints the walls in all the colours of the rainbow, there are ideas in the book to inspire all personality types and ages from newborn to school age. Be prepared to reap the rewards, not just in terms of school tests. It's likely you will begin to watch your child form better relationships, overcome challenges more confidently and simply become happier.

Perhaps the best part of all about unlocking your child's creativity though, is that you'll need to use your own imagination to unlock your child's creative potential, and that in itself can make life more fun and inspiring for the whole family.

As leading psychologist and expert in creativity Mihaly Csikszentmihalyi puts it in his book *Creativity: Flow and the Psychology of Discovery and Invention*, (HarperCollins, 1996):

> *Creativity is a central source of meaning in our lives. Most of the things that are interesting, important, and human are the result of creativity. What makes us different from apes – our language, values, artistic expression, scientific understanding, and technology – is the result of individual ingenuity.*

> *When we're creative, we feel we are living more fully than during the rest of life. The excitement of the artist at the easel or the scientist in the lab comes close to the ideal fulfilment we all hope to get from life, and so rarely do.*

Put simply, creativity makes all our lives more magical and meaningful.

1

....

How does nurturing creativity help my child?

In this chapter you will learn:
- *what creativity is*
- *how creativity is measured by psychologists*
- *how enhanced creativity can improve child development, well-being and happiness.*

This chapter will explain what creativity is, and why it's often expressed in very different ways from the artistic, musical and theatrical activities that are traditionally associated with creative talent. You will also discover how creative abilities vary, and the ways in which psychologists go about measuring a child's current level of creativity.

Finally, there will be a summary of everything you and your child stand to gain from following the tips in this book to enhance their creativity. You'll discover how studies have revealed that encouraging creative thinking and behaviour not only improves children's cognitive, social and physical development, but hugely improves their levels of happiness throughout their lives.

What is creativity?

Think of creativity, and we think of painters, poets and composers. And yet creativity is not simply the ability to draw a beautiful picture or play a perfect sonata on the piano.

More importantly creativity is the process, not the actual product. It is the generation and development of an original idea or thought, and the mysterious spark of inspiration which makes a piece of music or a new invention truly remarkable. Leonardo Da Vinci may have demonstrated enormous technical skill in his portrait of the Mona Lisa, but it is her cryptic smile, and the mystery which lies behind it which makes this painting the masterpiece which has stood the test of time.

Of course, it's unlikely that your child will come up with original ideas and solutions that no one has ever thought of before. No doubt other children have decided to paint the sky purple or wear their bobble hats on their toes in the past, but they are demonstrating creativity simply by dreaming up something new and original *to them*, or in that particular situation. Sometimes creativity is about asking questions no one has thought to ask before, challenging the things that the majority of us take for granted, and then having the curiosity and passion to seek out a novel solution. At it's simplest, creativity is all about individual response and expression – not following the pack or obeying the norm.

ARE ALL CHILDREN CREATIVE?

Just as some children are naturally fast to learn a language or to develop physical skills such as walking and running, children also have varying levels of natural creative ability from an early age. Having said this, however, psychologists believe that all children possess huge amounts of creative potential. What can often happen is that the potential is suppressed, rather than nurtured, often by very well-meaning adults. Consequently, it is very important for parents and carers to understand the creative process in all its different forms so we can help our children to maximize their creative potential.

Insight
As Pablo Picasso said: 'All children are artists. The problem is how to remain an artist once he grows up.'

Here we explore some myths and facts about creativity.

MYTHS ABOUT CREATIVITY

Myth 1: You have to be artistic to be creative

What's important to understand straight away is that you can find that magical spark that causes us to create something new and original in all professions, walks of life and day-to-day activities.

Creativity is about the ability to express yourself and to dream up ideas and questions which are groundbreaking and original. And it's not just artists, musicians and writers who possess this gift.

In science, for example, creativity is vital if experts are to break out of the boundaries of what we know and discover more about how the world works. Isaac Newton demonstrated amazing creative spark when he asked the legendary question 'Why does that apple fall to the ground?' It took a truly original thought process to question an ordinary, everyday occurrence which had been taken for granted for centuries.

Albert Einstein argued that 'imagination is more important than knowledge'. In his development of theories which dramatically altered our understanding of the universe and provided new insights into the birth of the universe and time travel, he demonstrated the truth of his statement beautifully.

The mathematicians who broke the Enigma code, the prehistoric inventor of the wheel and the first astronomer who dared to imagine that the world was round, all demonstrated remarkable feats of creative talent simply because they challenged assumptions, asked unusual questions, and thought about things in a very different way to the way that people had thought about things before.

Creativity has also helped us to make huge leaps forward in other areas too. In sports, this is true quite literally. In 1968, an athlete called Dick Fosbury attempted the high jump by throwing himself headfirst and backwards over the bar. This creative approach to an athletic event, although perplexing for many spectators, enabled him to win a gold medal and established his technique as a universal one for all future high jumpers. Although dramatic, this is certainly not an isolated example of the value of creative skills in sports. In football, for example, the best players are frequently described as excelling in 'creative play'. This is demonstrated clearly by the footballer who can neatly pass the ball to a teammate by aiming at a spot his opponents had not anticipated, or the manager who can introduce an innovative tactic to increase the team's chances of scoring goals.

Whether your child is an architect, nurse or car salesman of the future, encouraging them to think and behave in a creative, imaginative way from their earliest years will help them to achieve greater professional success as adults.

Top tip
In every line of work, from cleaning floors to running a multinational business, the ability to create new solutions to problems and to dream up new ways of doing tasks will help you to do that job better.

Insight
Some of the world's most successful businesses were launched on the back of innovative ideas which transformed the way we do everday things. A classic example is James Dyson, who invented a vacuum cleaner which didn't need bags.

Myth 2: Creative people are geniuses
Think of creative people and most of us think of Mozart, Picasso or possibly Einstein. We tend to think of people who have revolutionized our way of thinking and produced groundbreaking work that has changed the way the world works.

But on a less grand scale, most of us demonstrate some creative expression in our everyday lives. When you put together a brand new outfit for the first time, when you try a new route to get to work or throw together what's left in the fridge to make a new recipe, you're being creative. Sometimes our efforts at creativity are unsuccessful: the outfit looks terrible, you get stuck in traffic or the dinner is dreadful. But it is this sprinkling of daring and imagination that adds colour and novelty to our lives and helps us to break free of boundaries and constraints that limit us. Every so often we discover a beautifully flattering new suit, we find a way to work which is 15 minutes faster than our previous route, or we make an amazing new dish. Not only do we make our lives a little better, but we gain immense satisfaction from the creative process involved in doing so.

This is even more true for young children who are seeing the world with new eyes. Many adults think it is silly behaviour when a child asks why we wear socks on our feet, or spends hours happily throwing pebbles into a puddle so they can see how far the ripples move. But it is this childlike ability to look at things in new ways, to ask the questions no one else has thought of and to challenge the assumptions that adults no longer question which define the essence of creativity.

Myth 3: Creativity is a gift you are born with

To some extent this is true. Psychologists have been attempting to define and measure creativity in children since the 1950s and during that time they have made many discoveries. Perhaps the key discovery is that creativity and other forms of intelligence are independent of each other. A child who scores well in IQ tests will not necessarily score well in tests designed to measure creativity, and vice versa. The classic study which illustrates this was carried out in 1962 by Dr Jacob Getzels and Dr Philip Jackson, authors of *Creative Intelligence* (John Wiley & Sons), where the researchers found that IQ is not an accurate predictor of how creative a person is. This is particularly true in very clever children. The research found that if a child has an IQ of 120 or more, IQ was a very unreliable predictor of how creative someone is. This is not to say that someone cannot be very clever in the traditional sense and also creative – simply that averagely intelligent children can be highly creative, whereas highly intelligent children are not necessarily very creative.

The study has been replicated many times and is widely accepted by psychologists in the field of creativity. Whether creative talents are due to nature or nurture is the subject of debate. As with most things, the current thinking is that it's a blend of the two. Some children seem to be outstandingly creative from a very young age. Studies, such as those by educational psychologist Dr Frank Williams, author of *Creativity at Home and School* (Macalester College Press), have proved convincingly, however, that the way parents and teachers respond to children and the environments children spend time in hugely affect how creative they become. You certainly will play a very big part in how creative your child will become.

Myth 4: Creative people are absent-minded dreamers

The typical stereotype of a creative person is often that of someone who is slightly out of touch with reality, absent-minded and forgetful because they are constantly daydreaming.

There's a little bit of truth in this. Studies of highly creative people reveal that even as adults they tend to daydream. The stereotype is often reinforced because the creative process tends to involve periods when we dream and wonder about different possibilities, followed by a period of intense focus as a solution begins to take shape, where the creative person shuts out others and is likely to appear to be distracted and absent-minded.

But equally, studies also reveal that highly creative people also tend to be very self-disciplined and persistent. In his study of creative people, psychologist Dr Mihaly Csikszentmihalyi found creative people tend to combine playfulness with discipline. This is a key quality if someone is to move beyond the phase of dreaming to pulling thoughts together coherently and developing ideas so they can take shape and form and be expressed clearly. It's particularly true for people who are persistently creative, or who do creative jobs. They need to be able to develop ways of utilizing random ideas that flit into their heads. Many creative people are also very good at analyzing problems and discovering beautifully simple solutions. An urban myth which illustrates this well is that of the Russian scientists in the space race. The story goes that while NASA spent millions designing anti-gravity ballpoint pens that would work in space, the Russians simply sent the cosmonauts up with pencils.

Top tip
Sometimes the most sensible and most pragmatic children are actually incredibly creatively gifted.

Are some children more creative than others?

In a word, yes. Just as some children are quicker to walk or say their first words, some children are naturally more inclined to think in a creative way. Classic signs are that they'll connect seemingly random objects in a story, dream up strange new creatures to paint or think of numerous, very inventive games to play with the cardboard box that recently housed the new expensive toy you just bought them. Psychologists have spent decades researching creativity in children, and now there is a consensus on how to measure it and how to encourage it so those scores increase.

HOW IS CREATIVITY MEASURED?

The main term that psychologists use as a measure of a child's current scope to dream up ideas and think in an original way is something known as 'ideational fluency'. In simple terms, this is a measure of the quantity and quality of new ideas a child can come up with and how flexible their thinking is. This is tested in brainstorming exercises where children are asked to come up with different responses to different stimuli and questions. For example, preschool children may be asked to suggest as many things as they can think of that are round, or to come up with a list of different ways you can use a newspaper. The ideas the children come up with are measured in terms of number, originality and elaboration. Although scoring is complex, and there are several commonly-used tests, the general theme is that children who generate the highest number of original and elaborate ideas and those who are most flexible in their thinking are scored as being the most creative.

2-minute test

Ask your child to name as many things as they can that are red in 2 minutes. Answers such as cold noses, the sun at bedtime and daddy's face when he's running suggest a child is more creative than answers such as buses, traffic lights and strawberries, because they are more unusual and original.

However, just as psychologists know that we can increase our IQ through study and practical exercises, every child has the ability to increase and develop their creativity.

The Torrance Test of Creative Thinking

The most widely used test of childhood creativity is the Torrance Test of Creative Thinking, devised by Dr E. Paul Torrance. The test comes in two main forms, the Figural TTCT and the Verbal TTCT.

The Figural TTCT, thinking creatively with pictures, is most appropriate for use with young children and can be used from around the age of four or five. Children are asked to do three exercises involving pictures which measure the following five characteristics: fluency, originality, elaboration, abstractness of titles, and resistance to premature closure of the exercise.

The verbal TTCT is suitable for children aged six and over and in this test children are presented with imagined situations or objects and given the opportunity to ask questions, to improve products, and to 'just suppose'.

For example, a child may be asked to 'just suppose' that people could fly to the moon and to talk about some of the things that might happen if this were the case.

If you would like to try these tests on your child, you can order the tests online at www.ststesting.com/ngifted.html, or contact a local educational psychologist in your area. You can find a psychologist in your area at www.educational-psychologist.co.uk.

There are also some examples of the Figural and Verbal TTCT online at the University of Indiana Website at www.indiana.edu/~bobweb/Handout/d3.ttct.htm

---

Insight

Experts have found that creative people tend to use the right side of their brain more than the left side. This test at the Art Institute of Vancouver can tell you which side of the brain you prefer and how your way of thinking affects your creativity.

www.wherecreativitygoestoschool.com/vancouver/left_right/rb_test.htm

---

IS YOUR CHILD NATURALLY CREATIVE?

We tend to have a very narrow view of creative talent. Those who can draw a perfect apple, sing in perfect pitch or write a grammatically perfect story are often those credited with creative ability. But these are more proof of technical skills rather than creative skills.

Your child may not be particularly interested in the arts, or naturally gifted at the technical skills required for drawing or singing in perfect pitch. Instead, they might express creative flair more naturally in inventive plays on the football pitch, or through the ability to hold a captive audience when telling stories about the day at school. The truth is, as a society, we don't define creativity in children particularly well, and as parents we are often unaware of what to look for. Frequently, the signs of creativity are mistaken for naughtiness or childish eccentricity. If your child is frequently ticked off at school for daydreaming or asks very off-the-wall questions, such as 'Can stars make wishes too?' these are all signs of their natural creative talents.

Signs your child may be creatively gifted

THEY'RE OFTEN LOST IN DAYDREAMS

A vivid imagination, and a love of fantasizing and being playful with thoughts is a strong sign of a creative child.

THEY CONNECT SEEMINGLY RANDOM OBJECTS AND IDEAS IN THEIR FANTASY PLAY

Of course most children love imaginary play, but a key thing to look out for is if your child connects seemingly random objects or ideas into their play or stories. For example, they are an alien descending to sample the tomato soup on planet Earth, or their pretend horse loves chatting to the flowers on his mobile phone. This ability to make unusual connections is a key trait of very creative children.

THEY ASK LOTS OF UNUSUAL QUESTIONS

Most children go through a phase of asking 'Why?' to everything. But if your child is always asking questions and especially if he or she comes up with very strange, seemingly silly questions such as, 'What would happen if the sun came back up at night-time?' or 'Why don't apples grow from our fingers?' it is a strong sign they are very creative. What they are also demonstrating is the ability to rearrange elements of thought to create new ideas and the inclination to question things others take for granted.

THEY'RE OFTEN THE ODD ONE OUT; THEY DON'T DRESS OR ACT THE SAME WAY OTHERS DO

It's natural for children to want to be accepted by their classmates and friends, but some children will deliberately choose to be the odd one out no matter how much pressure there is to fit in. Often this is simply because they think differently to others, and thinking differently is thinking originally.

Kerrie, mum to Frankie, three

'Frankie's certainly got a mind of her own. At a party recently, she adamantly refused to dress up as a princess with the other girls and she insisted on dressing as a dinosaur in the Nativity play rather than play the part of one of the angels.'

Insight

Frankie's story dents another common myth people hold about creative people, which is that they are very shy. It takes a great deal of courage and confidence to be the only one who stands out from the crowd, and creative people often tend to spend time alone out of choice.

THEY'RE RESOURCEFUL AND GOOD AT SOLVING PROBLEMS

Creative children are, by definition, good problem solvers because they are flexible in the way they think and adapt quickly to different situations. Also, by definition, children who are creative will have lots of ideas and potential solutions to problems.

THEY LOVE PLAYING ALONE AND CAN ENTERTAIN THEMSELVES FOR LONG PERIODS OF TIME

Of course, children need some organized activities, and there's even some evidence that a little carefully selected TV can stimulate learning and ideas. But a child who's naturally able to come up with ideas is usually able to find plenty to occupy him or herself. In fact, it is very hard for children who are shuttled from one arranged activity to another, or put in front of the TV for long periods every day, to be creative.

THEY'RE OFTEN SO ABSORBED IN WHAT THEY'RE DOING, THEY DON'T EVEN HEAR YOU

Being utterly absorbed in creative play or activities is to be in what famous psychologist Abraham Maslow labelled a 'peak experience'. This is the ability to 'become lost in the present'.

It's an important ability, particularly for young children who need constant supervision, because it allows them to free themselves from interaction and interruptions by others, while remaining in their presence, so they can really focus on their own thoughts, feelings and experiences. This is essential for creativity, because it allows children to form individual and original thoughts.

THEY'RE REBELLIOUS
Of course, sometimes this is simply bad behaviour, but the instinct to think for themselves and to be individuals will drive creative children to question parents, teachers and books. It is down to you and your innate knowledge of your own child to determine whether a demand to wear a ballerina costume to bed is an act of creative expression, or a ploy to put off bedtime...

THEY ARE OFTEN BOTH EXTROVERTS AND INTROVERTS
Psychologists have found that very creative people can often be very outgoing and very shy at different times, whereas most of the population are either one or the other.

Cathy, 37, mum to Anne, five

Anne is incredibly shy with new people, yet oddly her teacher says she loves reading in front of the class, and she loves performing on stage doing ballet. Her voice is either a whisper, or very loud. She reminds me of famous actors you hear about who are happy to bare their souls in front of thousands, but are very shy when you meet them in person.

How does creativity help children to develop?

Many psychological studies reveal that creativity isn't just helpful for toddlers in terms of them learning how to scribble or to name their colours. Creativity helps children to understand new ideas more quickly and to express themselves. It also helps them to understand more about themselves and the people and the world around them. Through this, they develop their social skills as well. Below is an outline of how creativity can help to enhance your child's development in a number of key areas.

COGNITIVE SKILLS

Cognitive skills are basically the skills we use to learn something new and to understand it. These skills are obviously key throughout life, but are vital for young children at the preschool stage when they are learning at a vastly faster pace than adults. The process of cognition is that in being taught something, we think about it, we talk about it in our own words and then we notice how it relates to other things we know about. Because creativity helps children to think about and express things in new ways, for example to link warmth to the colour red, or the emotion of anger to loud noises, it means that they are more likely to find ways of thinking about the information which helps them to understand it more fully.

SELF-EXPRESSION

Whether your child is three or 13, they can find it immensely hard to convey their emotions and thoughts. A four-year-old may not be able to tell you they are sad, but they can make a painting of their house in blues and blacks and greys. And a 13-year-old may find it hard to cope with the feelings that come with moving to a new town, but through writing a story about someone else going through the same experience, they can start to understand their emotions and find ways to relay them.

Insight

If your young child is going through a difficult time and seems to find it difficult to express their feelings, suggest they do a drawing about how they feel. It will help them to express what they cannot find the words for and you can then name the feeling for them – anger, sadness or frustration, perhaps. They will also remember the drawing when they experience the feeling again and they will remember the name and words you used to explain it.

SOCIAL SKILLS

Because creativity allows self-expression, the next natural step is to begin to see how others are expressing themselves. Through music, dance or stories, children can begin to understand the thoughts and feelings of others, and then to respect them.

PHYSICAL DEVELOPMENT

Dance, of course, is the most obvious physical expression of creativity. But encouraging your child's imagination can lead to a host of other physical developments. It takes speed and agility to be Batman in the playground, and fine motor skills to draw a straight line in a picture. Understanding that you can exercise your imagination as well as your body by inventing new tactics on the football pitch can make PE a lot more exciting for children who are more creatively than physically inclined.

INTELLECTUAL SKILLS

Often, creative thinking is problem solving, but also solving problems that we never imagined were there in ways we hadn't thought of before. The skills we use in deciding which colours to use on a blank piece of paper, which character is about to be killed off in a story, or which block shapes to build with, help children to become more adaptable and flexible in their thinking and more innovative and less constrained when working out solutions and identifying problems in the first place.

GENERAL KNOWLEDGE

As well as developing all these other skills, creativity is often simply a fun way for your child to learn more about the world around them. The child who loves painting will soon come to understand that mixing blue and yellow makes green, and a child who enjoys music will learn bigger instruments tend to make deeper notes than smaller ones.

BEING HAPPY

To add to the list of life-enhancing qualities that creativity can give to our children, is the fact that children who do exercise their imagination and creativity are simply happier throughout their lives.

A key area of research is the theory of flow as developed by Mihaly Csikszentmihalyi, author of *Talented Teenagers: The Roots of Success and Failure* (Cambridge University Press) and a pioneer in the field of research in happiness and creativity. Flow, is a state of being so engaged and enraptured by the activity you are doing that you become lost, the 'self' disappears. These are our moments of true happiness.

This complete immersion in an experience could occur while you are singing in a choir, dancing, playing bridge, or reading a good book,' explains Csikszentmihalyi. 'Moments such as these provide flashes of intense living against the dull background of everyday life.

Although creative activities aren't the only times that we tend to enter this mystical state of happiness, Csikszentmihalyi's detailed surveys found that flow generally occurs when a person is doing favourite activities such as listening to music or cooking a good meal – the kind of pursuits which engage our creative thoughts if we do them with passion and enthusiasm. Very rarely do people report flow in passive leisure activities such as watching television.

10 THINGS TO REMEMBER

1 *Just because your child does not enjoy traditional arts such as music or painting, it does not mean they are not creative.*

2 *Creativity is about novel and individual expression. This can be expressed in jokes, on the sports field and countless other ways.*

3 *We are all creative in small ways, every day. Choosing our clothes, deciding the best route to work and writing emails are all creative activities and we can change our lives for the better by questioning whether we could do day-to-day things in a newer, better way.*

4 *We are all more creative as children than we are as adults, but some children are more creative than others.*

5 *Children can increase their natural creative abilities if parents and teachers respond to them in certain ways and if they spend time in an environment which encourages creativity.*

6 *A child who has a high IQ is not necessarily creatively gifted.*

7 *Basic tests of creative 'IQ' involve measuring the number and originality of ideas a child can come up with as well as the flexibility of their thinking.*

8 *Being creative helps children to learn more quickly.*

9 *Creative art forms such as music or drawing can help very young children to express and understand their feelings.*

10 *Creative people have more happy moments in their lives than people who aren't very creative.*

How to nurture creativity

In this chapter you will learn:
- *the golden rules for encouraging creativity*
- *to understand of the creative process*
- *about common creative killers*
- *good day-to-day habits to encourage your child to be creative.*

Many of us instinctively understand some of the key golden rules about encouraging creativity. We understand that our child is likely to be more creative if we give them a cardboard box or a blank piece of paper and crayons than if we allow them to watch a lot of television or if we draw the picture for them. We also understand from personal experience that it is easier to come up with a solution or new idea if we have time and space to think, without too many distractions. But in the real world, children clamour to watch their latest favourite TV programme, and quiet space is constantly invaded by siblings or the vacuum cleaner. In this chapter we'll examine practical ways to implement the 'Golden Rules' for encouraging creativity and identify lesser known strategies to encourage your child's inventive instincts.

Golden rules

GOLDEN RULE 1: LET YOUR CHILD LEAD THE PLAY

When we think about helping to nurture our children's creativity, many of us imagine providing paper and paints and glitter at the table, or organizing an activity to make snowflakes out of paper, or perhaps teaching them how to make music or to dance. But the latest research suggests that although it's good for us to provide interesting objects and materials for children to play with, and to be on hand to help and play with your child, your child will be happier and more creative if you allow time for unstructured play – in other words, you sometimes need to take a step back and let your child decide what they want to do.

Your child will need access to resources to encourage play and so it is a good idea to set out several different toys and materials which they can use as and when they wish during their playtime. Because they have initiated the play, they will be more actively engaged in whatever activity they are doing and as a result, they will learn more from it. For example, if you set out the paper plates, glue and paints and glitter, it is best to put it out, sit back, and let your child decide how to use the materials, rather than asking them to make a replica of a decorated plate you make yourself.

Allowing your child to lead their own play is not the easy option. Painting and crafts can certainly be messy and after all your careful preparation you may find your child is more interested in playing with teddy bears. This can be very frustrating, however, remember that your child is going to be more creative if they are making more choices about how they use the resources they're provided with.

Top tip

Under the standards set out in the UK's Early Years Foundation Stage, childcare providers are required to ensure that there is a balance of adult-led and child-initiated activities. The guidelines on adult involvement in play advise intervening occasionally when it is appropriate and making sensitive observations, but generally allowing plenty of time and space for your child to choose their own play activities.

'I spent a long time trying to persuade my four-year-old son Jack to make a leaf collage with paper and glue but he was much more interested in playing with his toy garage. Eventually, I just left the materials on a little table for him to use if he wanted to. A short while later, he went over to the table and made the most lovely shape of a tree, with a moon made from yellow leaves shining above it. Jack didn't choose to glue the leaves to the paper though, instead he arranged them all neatly on the carpet. He wanted to make a picture, but he wanted to make it his way.'

Insight

Creative things are not always things you can display on the wall or keep for any length of time, as Sarah discovered. In fact, as your child grows older, you should always ask if they are ready to share anything creative they've been attempting, and certainly check their feelings before showing it to others. Your child's confidence might plummet if their early attempts at poetry or singing are ridiculed by a sibling or criticized by a well-meaning adult.

GOLDEN RULE 2: LET YOUR CHILD DECIDE WHERE TO PLAY

When we think of where we carry out creative activities with children, the usual choice is to sit up at the table. For some activities this is sensible, it's difficult to glue if you are on the floor. But, if you think about where your child chooses to play most of the time, you quickly realize that preschool children often prefer to play on the floor rather than at the table. Not only is it more comfortable for them, but younger babies especially develop muscles and motor skills which help them to look up, roll and sit with improved posture when they are allowed to play on the floor.

Your child may often prefer to play outside too. Obviously this does depend on the weather to some extent, but there's no doubt that the sights, sounds, smells and textures of the natural world provide wonderful stimuli to encourage creativity in your child.

GOLDEN RULE 3: DON'T IMPOSE UNNECESSARY RULES

We all need some rules of course. Rules help to keep children safe and teach them how to behave in a considerate and thoughtful way. Many parents, however, instinctively impose rules on children which aren't strictly necessary, and when it comes to fostering creativity, it is vital to carefully consider rules before you impose them.

For example, a classic rule which stifles children's creativity is that they must colour in between the lines. It is a good rule if you're trying to teach fine motor skills and encourage your child to follow instructions carefully, but when it comes to encouraging them to express themselves and 'think outside the box', it quite literally reins in their natural creativity. Sometimes the rules we set can inadvertently impose our judgements on whether a creative effort is 'good' or not. At other times, we impose unnecessary limits which restrict a child from really letting go and experimenting freely with the new materials and inventive techniques.

Sarah, mum to Claire, two and a half

'I came across a really clear example of this the other day in the park. Claire was drawing shapes in the sandpit when another child came along and began to copy her. Her mum came along and was quite insistent about the fact that the sandpit was for making sandcastles. It was quite sad to watch the little girl, who had been drawing wonderfully swirly dolphin shapes, give up her game and obediently fill her bucket with sand.'

GOLDEN RULE 4: DON'T HELP TOO MUCH

Following on neatly from this example, is the importance of balancing your need to teach with the need to sometimes step back and let your child simply get on with what they are doing. There are times when they do need to be taught a technical skill so they can broaden their skills and try new things, for example, how to use safety scissors to cut paper. But the key crime of parents in stifling creativity is to step in and interfere when it is not necessary.

You might feel frustrated that your child can't quite get the hang of painting in separate colours yet and insists on mixing all the paints into the same sludgy brown shade. But aside from the fact that it is their picture and not yours, they learn from mixing up those colours, that blue and yellow makes green, that green and red makes brown, even if the end of their experimental splatterings is the inevitable mossy brown smudge all over the page.

Children need to experiment. And sometimes when they do it 'wrong', they come up with things that are surprising, delightful and truly inventive.

Jenny, mum to Maisy, four

'The other day when my daughter was putting her jumper on, she kept putting it on inside out. Then, suddenly, even though she'd put her head through the wrong way, and her arms too, she flipped it down so it ended up the right way round. She has actually found a brand new way of putting on her jumper which works, even though it isn't "right".'

....

Insight

Sometimes getting things wrong can lead to brilliant inventions. Things we have come to know and love that were created as the result of mistakes include chips, Frisbees and Post-it notes.

....

GOLDEN RULE 5: PRAISE THE PROCESS, NOT THE RESULTS

If your child runs to you proudly presenting a new painting or model they've made, it's any parent's natural instinct to offer praise.

No one is suggesting you give an honest critical appraisal of your three-year-old's attempt to draw Daddy, but studies do reveal that it's important to word your praise very carefully. It is only polite, of course, to say thank you when your child presents you with their latest artwork, however, over-enthusiastic praise can be unhelpful.

Studies carried out by psychologist Professor Wulf-Uwe Meyer from the University of Bielefeld, Germany, reveal that from a very young age children are very cynical about whether praise is genuine or not. His studies found that by the time they reach primary school, children can become cynical to the point where they no longer really believe any praise and therefore truly genuine appreciation begins to lose its value.

Another vital rule is to focus on praising the creative process rather than the creative product. Well respected studies by psychologist Dr Carol Dweck, author of *Mindset: the new psychology of success* (Ballantine), suggest that telling your child they are really talented or clever reinforces the message that attributes such as cleverness and creativity are things which are fixed and unchangeable. This kind of praise also conveys the idea that your child's natural creative talent is what you value them for, and this can build a fear of failure. Children become afraid to do something creative in case it isn't judged as being 'good' because that means that they are therefore not creative, and by default, less valued. In creative activities in particular, where work is often of a very personal nature, this can make children afraid to experiment and innovate.

To help your child understand that their creative work will become better with practice, Dweck says that you should take care to praise the effort and the process of doing the work, rather than commenting on the results. 'For example, tell them you really love the colours they chose in this painting, or that you know how hard they worked on their guitar practice to make that song sound so beautiful,' says Dweck. Dweck's 10 years' worth of studies, examining the gradual change of problem-solving abilities in groups of children given specific types of feedback, show that if you focus on praising the process in a sensitive yet honest way, your child is far more likely to feel confident in the creative work they do, to recover from setbacks and enjoy what they are doing.

Top tip

This is one example of how Dr Carol Dweck and colleagues tested the influence of feedback on children's problem-solving abilities.

Firstly, children were divided into groups and asked to do a simple puzzle. At first, researchers used just one line of praise to see how sensitive they were to the feedback. The first group were told they were clever to have done the puzzle so well, the second were praised for the effort they put in to solve the puzzle.

The next stage of the study continued with a harder puzzle, which the first group were much less willing to try to work on. Finally, they were given a puzzle of the same level of difficulty as the first again. The group praised for their effort rather than intelligence improved their score by 30 per cent while those praised for intelligence dropped their score by 20 per cent.

'Ultimately the way you praise doesn't just affect how confident your child is' says Dweck, 'but also how intelligent or skilled they will become.'

GOLDEN RULE 6: RESPECT YOUR CHILD'S PRIVACY

Just as the thought of showing someone a piece of creative writing, or sharing an unusual idea might make us a little nervous, sharing new ideas and thoughts can feel a little frightening for children too. This is especially true in their early years when they are still very much dependent on the approval of adults around them.

While they are working on something new, children need time and a private space where they can make mistakes and try new things without any risk of their efforts being judged, until they are ready to show you. And when they do, it is important to understand that despite any bravado or feigned indifference, often children care very much about how you react. At its heart, creativity of any kind is an intensely personal expression. It reveals that this is something the person has spent time and energy thinking about, that this is something important to them. Inevitably, it is an expression of the effort, talent and ability that went into it. When you hold up something you've created for judgement, you hand over a small piece of yourself. If you want to encourage creativity, it is important that a child is given private time and space to play and experiment with their expression, without the risk of ridicule or disinterested dismissal.

GOLDEN RULE 7: MAKE YOUR CHILD FEEL SAFE

The emotional stability of the world you create for your child will have a huge effect on how creative they are. Long-standing research reveals children need emotional stability before they begin to express themselves.

What the experts say: Why children must feel safe to be creative
In his classic work, psychologist Abraham Maslow set out what is termed as a 'Hierarchy of Needs'. His theory is generally illustrated as a pyramid, setting out the different kinds of needs people must meet before they can move up to the next level. At the very bottom, we must meet our physical needs – to be warm, fed and safe. Moving up the pyramid, we then have to meet our basic psychological needs – to be loved, and have a sense of belonging and to feel confident. Only when all of these needs are met, according to Maslow, can we begin to be creative, spontaneous and solve problems.

Making sure our children are warm, fed, safe and loved is something that most parents do as a matter of course. But by doing these things, and by paying careful attention to your child when they seem anxious and doing your best to reassure them that they are safe and protected, you are instinctively playing a huge part in nurturing their creativity.

GOLDEN RULE 8: TREAT YOUR CHILD WITH RESPECT

Children do need to know that they must obey certain rules and do what they're told in order to be safe and well cared for. There is a difference, however, between ensuring rules and routine are followed and undermining confidence by not showing simple levels of respect to children. Many adults, for example, talk down to children inadvertently, or talk about them in the third person when they are in the room. Children learn to understand long before they can speak, and so even before your child can really respond sensibly, you can encourage their confidence by genuinely asking for his or her point of view and by talking to them in the same tone that you would use if you were talking to an adult.

GOLDEN RULE 9: YOU CAN'T IMPOSE CREATIVITY

Famous psychologist Lev Vygotsky announced that creativity should not be imposed, and many researchers and experts would argue that it's virtually impossible to enforce real creativity. For every classical violinist who took up lessons at the age of three and excelled, there are many young children whose enthusiasm for a creative pursuit has been dampened by over-enthusiastic parents. Freedom to experiment and do things at their own pace is vital if children are to be truly creative. Provide them with opportunities, be there to help and encourage them, but don't be pushy.

GOLDEN RULE 10: REMEMBER CREATIVITY ISN'T ALL PAINTBRUSHES AND MOZART

At its core, creativity and self-expression meet a basic human need for self-fulfilment, and individuals find that creative fulfilment in all kinds of ways, not just in the arts and obvious creative outlets. While you might be at peace with the world when you're painting or listening to music, your child might experience the same sense of well-being while doing a jigsaw or finding new ways to organize the toys in the toy box.

GOLDEN RULE 11: LET THEM HAVE FREE TIME

This may seem an odd rule for preschool parents, but in a world where toddler ballet classes happen at the weekend and babies start yoga class when they are six weeks old, 'over-scheduling', as it's been named, is rife even in very young children. Having time and space just to think, play alone and just 'be' are vital to the creative process in children and adults. Don't feel like a bad parent if you leave your child to play on their own for an hour or two in the day, it's actually very good for them to do this. In fact, the standards set out for childcare providers by the Early Years Foundation Stage in the UK recommend that adequate time is allowed for children to enjoy unstructured play every day.

Finding the time

One issue that many modern parents find particularly difficult is how to find the time to encourage and share creative play with their children. Many parents have to juggle childcare, long working hours and many other different roles and commitments. Parents might be so busy that they find it hard to simply enjoy bath time and a bedtime story with their children.

Even for parents who stay at home, the demands of caring for young children who need to be fed, changed and constantly supervised means there are very few moments to even think up ideas for creative play, let alone to actually organize and enjoy them. And when you finally do manage to set out paints or make some play dough, many young children have such a short attention span that even carefully planned activities last less than 15 minutes.

However, you can do a good deal to nurture your child's creativity in very short spaces of time. In fact, often less is more when it comes to parental input into children's creative play. The child who draws pictures on the steamed up window of the car is enjoying the opportunity to be far more inventive than the child whose father sits down and meticulously guides him through every phase of building a cardboard spaceship.

Make use of the moments you have together, as you wait in a queue, or as you drive to playgroup, to play silly games or share funny stories. Even the time it takes to dry your child after a bath can be enough time to hear their latest song or funny joke.

Ask your child to make up a story and add a little bit every day in the car, or get them to think about everything they smelled today when you talk about their day at bedtime. And if you don't have time to physically sit down and glue together an elaborate spaceship with them, just giving your child six empty toilet roll holders to play with will keep their imagination active and happy for at least the time it takes for you to vacuum the living room.

> ## Top tip
> Having fridge magnets of different shapes and objects can give them the chance to make mess-free pictures while you load the dishwasher.

Letting them build things with plastic cups on the kitchen floor while you cook the evening meal is another way to keep them safe, happy and creative without you having to be a super parent. Ultimately, making the best use of the limited time you have involves you exercising your own imagination and resourcefulness.

Common creativity killers

We all try to be perfect parents, but sometimes our best intentions can backfire without us even realizing it. Here are some common habits which can stifle your child's desire and ability to be creative.

CREATIVITY KILLER 1: HELPING

Young children often find it frustrating when they are learning something new. They can't quite work out how to make their tree look right, or they hold the pen the wrong way up. But it pays dividends to sit back and let them carry on with whatever they are trying to do. If you insist on showing them exactly how to draw a tree, you're denying them the opportunity to find their own way of drawing it, and to experiment and learn things on their own. You're also inadvertently setting them up for failure – their tree isn't going to be as good as yours, they are not going to be able to use a pen as easily as you. This can make them feel even more frustrated. Your child will only gain confidence if you give them the opportunity to prove to themself they can do some things without your help.

CREATIVITY KILLER 2: THE WRONG TOYS

Most houses have them, the toys with bright colours, flashing lights, a variety of songs and perhaps some Beethoven to help them learn the alphabet. Toys like these are fun, and have their benefits, but in terms of encouraging your child to be imaginative, they are creativity killers. Most parents have had the experience of their child abandoning the expensive toy for the box it came in at Christmas, but few of us learn from that. Children really do stretch their imaginations further if they are making up their own songs, or playing with a cardboard cut-out sword rather than a flashing light sabre.

CREATIVITY KILLER 3: DECIDING WHAT IS RIGHT AND WRONG

By telling a child the 'right' way to paint the rainbow, or that it's 'wrong' when they bang all the keys on the piano at once, you are limiting your child's early experiments. Picasso's cubist artwork did not fit with the aesthetic standards of conventional art at the time and modern classical music might seem out of key and harsh to most listeners. Yet art and music critics have come to applaud these expressions of creativity which fall outside the norm by conventional standards. Creativity is all about thinking outside the normal rules and dreaming up new ways of doing things. This is exactly what your child is doing when he draws the world upside down or when she colours the sea pink.

Insight

Do you think your child's paintings are as good as anything you'd see in a modern art gallery? You may be right. Picasso once commented: 'It took me four years to paint like Raphael, but a lifetime to paint like a child.'

CREATIVITY KILLER 4: PLANNING THEIR TIME

Children definitely need routine and structure in their day, but do be wary of planning your child's time too rigidly. Try to allow time each day for 'unstructured play' where your child can choose his or her own activities freely and, where possible, be a little flexible in cancelling other scheduled activities if your child is really involved in what they are doing. If your child is thoroughly absorbed, they are probably contented and learning a good deal.

CREATIVITY KILLER 5: RIGHT ANSWER SYNDROME

Children love to do things well and win approval, but beware of cultivating a need in your child to get things 'right'. One of the key traits of creative people is that they are good at 'divergent thinking', which means they can suggest lots of different potential answers or solutions to a puzzle or question. Of course, sometimes there is only one right answer. But try to present your child with situations and tests where they can learn that sometimes there are lots of different correct answers, and that different people's responses are all equally valid.

CREATIVITY KILLER 6: COMPETITION

There is fierce debate amongst educationalists about whether competition is good for children. When it comes to creativity, however, studies such as those by Professor Teresa Amabile at Brandeis University suggest that competition can negatively influence creativity. Competition automatically infers that judgement is being made over the creative product, which can make the child less willing to take risks and be inventive. In addition, Amabile and many other psychologists argue that children should be encouraged to enjoy creativity simply because it is an enjoyable and fulfilling process, not as a means to win contests or rewards. Much research suggests that rewarding a child simply for doing something creative eventually lessens their interest in doing creative activities for which they are not rewarded.

Good habits to get into

▶ *Imaginary play with your children*
▶ *Making up silly stories*
▶ *Singing in public or at least in the car*
▶ *Dancing around the living room*
▶ *Sharing jokes*
▶ *Playing CD roulette to listen to new styles of music*
▶ *Asking questions*
▶ *Stopping to look at intriguing things*
▶ *Jumping in muddy puddles*
▶ *Spending time 'doing nothing'*
▶ *Describing how food tastes*
▶ *Tickling each other.*

10 THINGS TO REMEMBER

1 *Think before you step in to help your child. Are you stopping them from making a mistake, or stopping them from learning and trying something new?*

2 *Provide ideas and resources for your child but let them play the way they want to as far as is reasonably possible.*

3 *Children need to feel physically safe and secure and loved before they can be very creative.*

4 *All parents do their best to ensure their child is safe, but also think about how you can help them to feel safer. There may be no monsters under the bed but they will feel safer if you go and look together.*

5 *Don't give false praise but always thank your child and make positive comments about things that are good in things they have tried.*

6 *Try to focus praise on the effort that went into their achievements, as well as the results.*

7 *Make sure your child has some free time to do things they want to do every day.*

8 *If you are busy there are plenty of things you can do with your children to encourage their imagination which don't take much time, such as playing car games on the school run or swapping a daily joke.*

9 *Simple toys such as scarves to dress up with, tambourines or paper and crayons will do more to stimulate creativity than expensive and more sophisticated toys, which do things to entertain your child.*

10 *Don't reward your child for a creative achievement. They are more likely to become more creative if they learn to love it for the sake of doing it. Instead offer creative activities such as painting or music as a reward.*

3

How to make your home
a creative environment

In this chapter you will learn:
* *how you can adapt your home to encourage creativity for all the family*
* *ways to make your child's room more inspiring and practically set up for creative play*
* *what items make up a basic creative store cupboard.*

Our homes reflect our personalities and lifestyles, and whether yours is a minimalist haven of calm or a cluttered jumble of intriguing objects, decades of research reveals that our homes, as the environment where young children spend much of their time, have a huge influence on their early development.

In this chapter, you will find out how, with just a few simple changes, you can create an environment which really encourages and enables your child to be spontaneously creative. Decor plays a small part, but it is far more important to think about the spaces you create in your home and to take practical steps to ensure your child has access to simple resources and areas that will allow them to be more experimental and varied in their play.

You'll also discover more about the creative process, and the different phases children go through as they are being creative and examine how we can make simple alterations in our homes to allow for these different moods and phases.

You will find out about the importance of tidiness and order, discover clever tricks with layout that will make your child feel secure, but not smothered, and look at how the things you display in your home, such as pictures and art, can inspire or flatten creativity. Finally, you'll also look at day-to-day habits in the household routine which can help to foster creativity not just in the children, but in the whole family.

Ways to make your home a more creative place

1. GIVE YOUR CHILD A SPACE FOR QUIET TIME

One of the most effective things you can do to foster your child's creativity is to create a space in your home where they can have time, privacy and quiet space. But it doesn't have to be a whole room. In fact, having another space downstairs or in the general living area of your home is beneficial for young children. In this way, you can create a space where your child can enjoy personal space while remaining protected and supervised. According to well-known child psychoanalyst, Dr Donald Winnicott, this sort of area – known as 'a holding environment' – is extremely beneficial in helping young children to gradually develop independence and to play creatively.

In terms of practicality, your child's space needs to be somewhere they can sit quietly to read and play, away from distractions such as the TV or people walking to and from other rooms. It needs to be a corner, where you can discreetly observe them so that they feel and are safe and content, but which also gives them a sense of privacy so that they do not feel they are under constant surveillance as they practise drawing something new or talk to themselves about the book they're looking at.

Setting up cushions in a corner of the living room, behind a sofa, or placing a screen or shelf to create a separate corner in a room are all ways to create a good 'quiet' space. It helps if you can make the space somewhere you too can sit down and read aloud with your child. If a room is very small, decorating a fairly big cardboard box, or using a small pop-up tent to act as a removable 'den' is a good solution.

Before choosing this space, take a little time to observe how your child currently uses the spaces in your home. Sometimes children themselves naturally carve out their own areas, dragging toys, books or cushions to a special spot which they are drawn to.

Claire, mum to Joseph, one

'I created a reading corner almost by accident in my house. Obviously with Joseph being so little, I needed to keep an eye on him pretty much all the time so he couldn't have a totally private space. But I noticed that there was one corner of the kitchen where he'd go to sit with his toys or books while I was making tea. I cleared a little space there and put a small beanbag down, then cleared the shelf next to it and placed a basket there, filled with his toys and books. He doesn't stay there for very long periods, but he does love it there, especially when he needs some quiet time after he has been running around. He's started to call it "Jo's cushion" now. He knows it's somewhere he can go for a little time out, but still feel safe because I'm fairly close.'

2. GET THE RIGHT LIGHTING

Light in your home needs to fulfil two key functions. Firstly, there's the practical function of it being bright enough to read, write or draw in. But also, importantly, light affects the mood and atmosphere of a room. Whereas lots of bright natural light can be inspiring and encourage a sense of space and freedom, bright artificial lights can make you feel scrutinized and uncomfortable. In addition, bright light tends to increase our brain wave frequency to beta level, a level where we're alert and able to concentrate. However, in this light few people can relax enough for the brain to begin operating at the alpha waves frequency (between 7–12 HZ), which is the range we tend to operate at during the daydreaming and exploring phase of the creative process (see more about this later in this chapter).

Get the balance right by having muslin curtains or blinds to control the levels of natural light so enough pours into the room without it feeling overwhelming. In the evening, lamps or up-lighters create pools of light in areas where we can sit and read or work without lighting up every corner of the room and stopping us from relaxing.

Insight

The colour of the lights you use will have a big effect on your child's mood. When they need to rest, warmer pink or orange lights mimic twilight and help them to sleep. Brighter, bluer light will help them to wake after a nap and enjoy more alert, active play.

3. MAKE YOUR HOME MORE MUSICAL

Children love music, and it helps them to explore their feelings and creativity through dancing, rhythm, melody and language. At this young age, they love listening to all kinds of music and the more opportunities they get to hear it the better.

Make sure there is a space somewhere in your home where your child can dance around to some music. It may simply be clearing a space in the living room. If you do have an area where they can be noisy and dance and sing, it's also a good idea to keep a box of musical instruments such as maracas and tambourines here, and maybe some dressing-up clothes, feather boas, or scarves they can use while they are dancing.

Also pay attention to where the music area is. If the space is near the washing machine, or TV, it may limit opportunities for using it. Likewise, if the area is near to a baby's bedroom, or a home office, it may make your child uneasy about making noise and enjoying themselves.

Top tip

The best way to see if your music corner is working is to watch and see if your child uses it a lot, and if not, ask them why.

4. PAY ATTENTION TO TEXTURE

You might have painted your home in beautiful colours and have enchanting music playing most of the day. But one sense we often really neglect to cater for in our homes is our sense of touch. It's not just the bedroom where we need cushions, soft throws and other props to make us physically feel comforted and pampered. It's tempting to have a very utilitarian approach to soft furnishings and ornaments when you do have young children who break things and spill juice on throws most of the time, but with relatively cheap and indestructible objects and textiles you'll give your child the opportunity to explore and experiment with their sense of touch and add another dimension to your home.

When you set out toys and materials, try to include some which encourage them to explore their sense of touch, and make sure you have plastic sheets or an outside area for messy play. It helps if you also have plastic trays or a sand and water table where they can play freely with these materials and others such as mud, gloopy dough and finger paints.

Insight

According to experts (including Professor Yukuo Konishi of the Center for Baby Science at Doshisha University, Japan, the sense of touch is the very first sense we develop, and the sense of touch is vitally important to baby's development. Babies learn a lot about the world in their first year by touching things and putting them in their mouths, so keeping some safe, clean toys they can put into their mouths is useful.

5. MAKE SURE YOUR CHILD FEELS SAFE

Naturally, we make sure our child is secure at home. We take steps to ensure they can't run out into the road, and that they're unlikely to topple heavy objects or reach dangerous things. But making sure a preschool-aged child feels safe means trying to adjust the layout of your home so they can see or hear you, and know you're within shouting distance most of the time. It can be difficult to alter the layout of your home to accommodate this all of the time, but setting up a toy corner near the kitchen is helpful, or putting their toy box in a spot where they can hear you if you're in the next room. Another way to make your home feel friendlier and less intimidating to your child is to get down to their level and move through it. This will help you to see your home through your child's eyes and to spot things you wouldn't ordinarily notice, for example, the way the shelf in the living room completely blocks you from view when they're sitting by their book basket.

6. OUTSIDE SPACE

Not all of us are fortunate enough to have a large garden, but even a small outdoor space can be adapted to add a valuable element to your child's home environment.

The standards set out in the UK's Early Years Foundation Stage strongly recommend that young children have regular access to outdoor play. Playing outside means that children get to use all of their senses and to be physically active. They learn by moving, doing and exploring, and they learn about the weather, the seasons and nature as well. Children are also often allowed to be more energetic, noisy and messy when they play outside, so they enjoy a greater sense of freedom and independence.

If you can make even just a small area safe for your young child to play in, they will gain enormous benefits.

CASE STUDY

Joanna, mum to Fiona

'I found out while talking to my local playgroup teacher that nurseries are often encouraged nowadays to have "free flow" areas which means they have secure outdoor areas accessible from the classroom, so the children can go inside or outside when they like. It seemed like a fabulous idea, so, as Fiona was just two at the time, I copied the set up the playgroup had adopted, which was to fence off an area of the back patio with a special children's safety playpen that opened out into a room divider, which was adjustable to enclose spaces around doorways. I fixed two of those together to make a little backyard area where Fiona could play safely in a space where I could see her. Then I set up a little chair and table and some toys out there for her. I soon found she actually preferred to spend most of her time playing outside even on grey days.'

> **Insight**
>
> Make a little sensory garden area, which will allow your child to explore all five senses, by planting brightly-coloured flowers, rustling grass, herbs such as mint and lavender, and plants with soft leaves such as silver sage. For a guide on good plants to include (and which are safe) visit www.sensorytrust.org.uk and www.thekidsgarden.co.uk.

7. DISPLAY LOTS OF ART

Most parents have their children's sculptures, collages and pictures around the house, but creating a special area to display the works of which they are most proud will really make them feel that you value and respect what they've created.

Buying clip frames for their work, for example, is a cheap and pretty way to display pictures, and avoids the problem of paper curling, or being torn or damaged. By being selective, you're also showing genuine rather than scattergun praise, which makes the act of displaying the work much more meaningful, even to smaller children.

By displaying things you yourself have created, or collected – for example, a few interesting photographs, prints and objects you love – you're encouraging your child to develop their own aesthetic and habitual appreciation of art and interesting objects and images. When you display photos you've taken, or interesting things you've collected, such as driftwood or shells, you are implicitly giving your child the message that it is a good thing to express your own creativity in your home.

8. HAVE A WRITING SPACE

Simply making sure there is somewhere your child can sit up to write or draw, and providing a ready supply of paper and writing implements means your child will be able to scribble and draw when the mood strikes them, rather than limiting them to doing these activities when you or another adult sets out the supplies.

9. BRING NATURE INTO THE HOUSE

Children love learning more about the natural world. Having pets may be difficult, but even a small fish tank will be really inspiring for some young children. An alternative is to set aside a small area where there are cuddly toy animals and books about animals and atlases. Also try to have some plants around the house. Encouraging your child to help you look after them, or to grow their own potted plants is another way to stimulate their interest and to encourage them to ask new and interesting questions about nature.

Top tip
Keep a nature detective box near the back door for expeditions into the garden or to your local park or woods.

(*Contd*)

Stock it with a magnifying glass, notepad and paper to scribble pictures, a book with pictures of local plants and animals, and plastic food bags to keep the things you collect on your nature trails.

10. HAVE A MATHS BOX

Maths might not seem to be a creative subject, but actually the problem solving and inventive thinking required for the subject means it is a very creative subject, as well as being an area which will help your child to develop academically. To help your child make interesting connections about early maths, make up a box with toys such as shape sorters, number books and counting games.

Insight
The Internet has many helpful websites which can give ideas and games to get children enjoying and understanding maths. Websites such as www.puzzlepixies.com and www.mathletics.co.uk have games and exercises for children from preschool age.

The creative process

In the last 50 years psychologists have come to understand that being creative generally involves going through several different key phases, all of which involve different moods and behaviour.

It's helpful when thinking about how a home can foster creativity to understand what these phases are for young children, so you can make sure there are places that suit each creative mood.

PHASE ONE: INTEREST AND CURIOSITY

Creativity begins when a child begins to become curious about something. This can be a toy, a sound, or a problem they cannot solve – anything in their environment which gains their interest and makes them begin to question.

> *In the home, setting out a selection of interesting objects and easily accessible toys and activities for your child, and rotating them regularly, will help to stimulate creative thinking.*

PHASE TWO: EXPLORATION AND PLAY

The next step is when a child begins to gather more information about the item, materials or situation. They may simply listen intently, or observe from a distance for a while. They may tap the ball to see if it rolls away again, or put their fingers in some glue to feel the texture, or ask lots of questions about a musical instrument. It is important to recognize this as part of being creative, and to allow plenty of time for it. Your child may not actually be in the process of inventing anything new, but the thought processes that could eventually lead them to do this cannot be hurried.

> *Ensure toys and materials are set out and stored so they are accessible for the child to leave and come back to. This will allow them to carry on exploring as the mood strikes them.*

Insight

The Internet is a valuable way for children to discover more about the world, to get new ideas and to enjoy all kind of resources that can inspire creativity. But you need to monitor them and be aware of safety issues. Websites such as www.kids.getnetwise.org/safetyguide and www.microsoft.com/protect/parents/childsafety/age.aspx have guidance for parents of children, organized by your child's age.

PHASE THREE: ILLUMINATION – OR, THE EUREKA MOMENT!

After initial curiosity and thought, the next big step in the creative process is 'illumination'. The story which often best describes this moment is that of the ancient Greek philosopher and scientist Archimedes, who suddenly understood an important scientific principle while enjoying a bath. The story goes that he leapt out of his bath shouting 'Eureka!' (I have it!). The moment of illumination is just this, the 'A ha!' moment when the penny drops and the child gets an idea about how to solve a problem, or an idea about what they are going to make.

Sometimes children might need some guidance as they approach this stage. Asking them to tell you what they are thinking out loud can help, or guiding them with questions they could ask themselves that might help them on their way. Typically, this is a moment marked by excitement and energy, but immediately before this moment your child might be tense and cross about interruptions. If you take your child away from the activity at this stage they are also likely to be very upset, because often the idea that was about to form is lost and the child has a sense that something has been 'taken away'.

> ▶ *Having your child's play areas in spaces where you can observe discreetly from a distance means you can observe when they are getting frustrated by a problem or activity and make appropriate interventions to help your child find his or her own answer.*

PHASE FOUR: ACTIVITY, CREATING SOMETHING

Finally, your child reaches the point at which they begin to make the product, or try out the solution which all the previous stages have led up to. Perhaps they have found a way to stop the den they have made from a bedsheet and chairs from falling down and are reconstructing it, or maybe they've suddenly thought of something they want to paint.

> ▶ *It's important for your child to have some privacy and somewhere they can leave half-finished experiments or pictures without feeling that they are going to be scrutinized. Also, the amount of noise and mess you allow sends out a strong message about how tolerant you are of risk and experimentation, so try to maintain a balance between chaos and restrictive levels of order and tidiness.*

Your child's room

Your child's room is the perfect space for them to express themselves and their changing sense of identity as they grow. Of course you'll need to set out rules to teach your child to respect their belongings and the work involved in decorating the space. But allowing them a choice in the colours, pictures and items on display is a wonderful way not only to encourage them to express themselves, but also to ensure that this is a space where they feel comfortable, secure and in control.

Other ways to encourage your child to be creative in their room include using blackboard paint for the walls or asking them to help you paint a mural which they can use as a backdrop to role play. They might also like to make things to go in their room, or to have a picture rail with pictures of people and things they love.

Another element that's important to your child's room becoming a haven of creativity is that you respect it is their private space. Obviously privacy is not appropriate for very young children who need to be supervised for safety reasons, but from as young as two or three, children begin to need some privacy, within reasonable limits. Having a room which they feel is very much their own and where they can relax and be their own person will make it much easier for them to have their own unique, original thoughts and feel confident in expressing them.

Insight

Take some time in your child's room to do some work or a hobby of your own so you can get an idea of good and bad things about the environment. For example, does the room feel calm and safe? Is there noise from the road or neighbours which you weren't aware of? How does the natural light change in the room throughout the day?

Your creative store cupboard

A well-stocked craft box makes it easier to be a bit spontaneous about setting up creative activities. Here's a list of items it is good to gradually gather together for your 'creative store cupboard' that will serve a multitude of purposes:

▶ *Musical instrument box: put together a box of maracas, tambourines, drums, or just household items such as old pans, and wind chimes.*

▶ *Dressing-up box: rather than having too many specific costumes, fill the box with items that can be adapted for lots of different scenarios – scarves, hats, strings of beads, toy phones, old shoes and scraps of materials are all good things to include. Then make sure there's a mirror nearby, or keep a safe plastic one in the box.*

▶ *Craft box: this could include: recycled plastic containers, cardboard boxes and tubes, glue, double-sided sticky tape, normal sticky tape, crayons, felt tips, pencils, paints, paintbrushes, glitter, paper and card, googly eyes, old magazines, coloured feathers, scraps of material and ribbons, pipe cleaners, stencils, balloons, rubber bands, string, bits of dowling, plastic cups, newspaper, pots containing buttons, bottle lids, or other collage materials. Ideally your child will help you sort and store these.*

▶ *In the kitchen: try to keep a store of natural food colouring, flour (plain and self-raising), butter and eggs, coloured icing, cookie cutters, cupcake cases, baking soda, cornstarch, glycerine, plastic trays, old plates or paper plates for paint pallets.*

Top tip

We all like to help and encourage our children, to get them to try new things and to guide them in their efforts to learn letters, numbers and colours. It's good to do this with your child, but do be wary of taking on too much of a teacher role at home with your child. Your child needs you to be someone they can sometimes curl up and be 'little' with, someone who will cuddle them, laugh with them, who they can make fun of and laugh with. The time you spend nurturing your child's creativity is as much about building the bond between you as parent and child as helping your child to develop new skills and abilities. Your home needs to reflect that too. Make sure that above all, your home is a place for fun, play and relaxation, not an extension of the classroom.

Creativity killers in your home

As with everything, it's a case of balance, but there are some things about your home you should be aware of that could make it a place that promotes rather than stifles creativity.

CREATIVITY KILLER 1: THE TV

A small and carefully monitored amount of TV can be inspiring and educational (Drs Dorothy and Jerome Singer, Yale Child Study Center), but many studies have shown that spending hours in front of the TV stunts creativity as well as academic and language development. One study by the Johns Hopkins, Bloomberg School of Public Health, found that children under five who watch more than two hours of television each day are at increased risk of behavioural problems and are more likely to exhibit problems with social skill development.

Take a look at where the TV is situated in your house. Does it dominate the main living space? Can you happily spend time in that room without switching it on? Is there a space you could move it to which would mean that not every family member had to watch it if it was switched on?

CREATIVITY KILLER 2: TOO TIDY HOUSES

It's not necessarily true that a cluttered, jumbled home is a more creative one. Too much clutter and mess can make many people feel tense and stressed. However homes where every surface has to remain spotless and where it's not easy for a child to pull out their books or toys can be intimidating. They can also be very sparse when it comes to objects that are interesting and accessible to children. According to Professor Tina Bruce, author of the book for child carers, *Cultivating Creativity in Babies, Toddlers and Young Children* (Hodder Education), the amount of noise and mess you allow also gives a clear indication to your child of how accepting you are of risk-taking and innovation. You need to achieve a balance. If you want and need your home to be pristine, allocate just one room or part of a room for play and relax the rules on mess in that area.

CREATIVITY KILLER 3: PUBLIC SPACE

We tend to have different spaces in our homes. We have the very private spaces, our bedrooms usually, and then areas where the family spend a lot of time together such as the living room and kitchen, these are the parts of our home where we will invite visitors and where friends and neighbours will come and spend time. Be aware of the different levels of spaces in relation to where your child's play area or room is. Your child will instinctively feel more secure if there is a little distance between their play space and the main public spaces and paths where visitors will enter and leave the house.

CREATIVITY KILLER 4: POOR STORAGE

It's simple, but often overlooked, If your child's toys are all jumbled up in an enormous wooden box, or out of reach, they'll end up playing with just a few, and won't be as spontaneous in their play. Storing books spine out isn't helpful to young children either, as they will find it hard to identify books easily. Often they will pull all the books out to find the ones they want to look at and if this results in them being told off, it will make reading a less enjoyable experience. Get a box or basket or shelf where you can stack books with the covers facing out, so your child can rifle through them easily.

CREATIVITY KILLER 5: PETS AND SIBLINGS

Younger children and pets frequently bring an abrupt halt to
creative proceedings by knocking over block constructions or
trying to draw on their older sibling's painting. If this happens
often enough it can make a child feel so frustrated that they
eventually give up their efforts. If possible, set up your child's
writing, or playing space so you can either watch and protect that
space from a distance or make the space beyond the reach of these
constant interruptions.

CREATIVITY KILLER 6: SURVEILLANCE

You do need to watch young children, but it is possible to do
this in a way that does not make them feel watched. Keeping
some distance and creating an area which you don't enter unless
your child needs or invites you can help to give your child a
good sense of freedom and privacy. Likewise, giving them a box
or basket where they know unfinished activities or creations can
be left until later will be helpful. It's important that you don't
go to look at these things or comment on them until your child
invites you to. They are more likely to take risks and experiment
if they don't feel that you might place judgement on their early
efforts.

Ways to add creative magic to day-to-day activities

It is possible to introduce creativity into the most mundane of
day-to-day activities. Not only does this encourage your child to
become more creative habitually, but it gives the message that
creativity doesn't have to involve making huge works of art and

demonstrates how imagination can bring a little magic into even the greyest day and make life more enjoyable.

- ▶ *Get your children to choose a 'play list' of their favourite songs each week for short car journeys.*
- ▶ *Play some fast music and encourage the children to do funny walks to it while they help you empty the dishwasher or put the shopping away.*
- ▶ *Give your vacuum cleaner a name and pretend you're giving him his dinner when you vacuum the house.*
- ▶ *Invent tidying games, for example, how many toys with wheels can you find to put in the toy box, who can get the most building blocks into the box from 2 metres away?*
- ▶ *Have role-play areas or make-believe toys in the same place as the real ones, for example, a play kitchen in the kitchen, toy cleaning sets in the cleaning cupboard, so your child plays along while you get on with jobs.*
- ▶ *Humour is a wonderful expression of creativity. Swap jokes with children and ask them if they've heard any new ones at the end of the day.*

Insight

A Harvard Medical School study revealed children laugh ten times more than adults, which is one reflection of how much more naturally creative they are. Studies by psychologist Alic Isen reveal we're much more creative after we've been laughing.

- ▶ *Have play time as well as washing hair time and cleaning time in the bath. And join in too. Make bubble beards and bubble hair, or pretend to be a newsreader with the side of the bath as your 'desk'.*

10 THINGS TO REMEMBER

1 *Create a space where your child can enjoy quiet time to read, draw or play alone safely, without feeling that they are 'under surveillance'.*

2 *Make sure that as well as being safe, your child feels safe in your home. For example, set their play area away from the area of the house where people come and go a lot, try to keep loud noises to a minimum, and if they are frightened of monsters under the bed, don't dismiss the fear but show them they aren't there.*

3 *Try to have some space in the main living area where someone can read, play or spend time if they do not want to watch the TV when it is on.*

4 *Express your own creativity in your home, whether that is by listening to music or displaying art or craftwork you've made or collected.*

5 *Encourage your child to be curious by introducing new things to your home often, such as a seasonal nature table.*

6 *'Making something' is only the final part of the whole creative process. Make sure that your child has time and space in your home to simply explore and play with a variety of resources, as well as providing materials for them to express their ideas.*

7 *Give your child a reasonable amount of privacy. Keep interruptions to a minimum when they're very absorbed in an activity and don't insist on seeing everything they do, while letting them know you'd love to see what they want to show you.*

8   *Give your child some say in how their room looks, so it becomes 'their' space.*

9   *Keep a general stock of basic art and craft materials, baking ingredients and dressing-up clothes, so that there are always a few options for spontaneous, creative play.*

10 *Allow a little bit of mess!*

4

Pregnancy to six months

In this chapter you will learn:
- *how to influence your child's creative talent during pregnancy*
- *how the nursery design can promote imaginative behaviour*
- *which toys and games promote creativity in babies from birth to six months.*

Many people are sceptical about just how much parents can help their baby's future development at this early stage in their lives. Yet increasingly, studies show that parents do have a strong influence on their child's future intellectual and creative abilities from before they are even born. In fact, parents can even begin this process before conception by adapting their diet to give a baby the best nutrition to ensure healthy brain stem development. For example, it is well established that folic acid reduces the risk of brain stem abnormalities during pregnancy. One recent study by Dr Emily Oken and colleagues, published in the *American Journal of Epidemiology* in 2008, revealed that eating a moderate amount of fish during pregnancy was linked to children scoring better in tests of cognitive abilities at the age of three.

In this chapter, you will discover what the latest studies say about how eating well and changing your lifestyle during pregnancy can affect your child's abilities in problem solving, learning and creativity as they grow older.

You will also learn how simple things such as the choice of colours in your child's nursery and the toys and games you play with your newborn can help your baby to become playful, curious and brave enough to try new things – the foundation of a creative and imaginative personality.

During pregnancy

It might seem improbable that you can influence your baby's intellectual, emotional and creative IQ before you have even conceived, but science reveals that you can make a difference. In fact, your baby might even have developed his or her brain stem, the foundation for all their thoughts, feelings and senses, before you're even aware you are pregnant – by week four.

YOUR BABY IS WHAT YOU EAT

Simply by ensuring your intake of folic acid is 400 micrograms in the weeks and months before conception, and between 600 and 1,000 micrograms during pregnancy, you are providing your baby with the building blocks to develop a strong, healthy neural tube, essential in the development of a healthy brain. Fortified breakfast cereals, lentils, beans and chicken are all excellent sources, and there are plenty of supplements available specifically designed for pregnant women.

Other foods are also linked to healthy development of the foetal brain during pregnancy. Recent research, such as that by Joseph Hibbeln of the National Institute on Alcohol Abuse and Alcoholism, reveals that despite warnings about the consumption of too much seafood during pregnancy, eating fish can improve your child's abilities to learn to talk, their fine motor skills and their social development. A study of over 10,000 British women revealed that researchers could measure this impact on children aged up to seven years old.

The idea that eating seafood can help enhance your unborn baby's creative talents is supported by other research which shows that an expectant mother's intake of omega-3 polyunsaturated fatty acids (PUFAs) is linked to her child's problem-solving abilities and attention span. Walnuts, flax seeds (and eggs of hens fed on flax seed) and seafood such as salmon, mackerel, tuna and scallops are all good sources of PUFAs.

Eggs can also play a huge part in your baby's healthy brain development. Studies (by Dr Gary Shaw, a research director of the California Birth Defects Monitoring Program and Dr Steven Zeisel, a recognized expert in choline) reveal that choline, a vitamin B-like compound which is also found in beef and chicken liver, wheat germ and soybeans, not only helps prevent neural defects but also has a strong effect on your child's ability to learn and remember things.

THE IMPORTANCE OF KEEPING CALM

As well as what you eat, research also reveals that trying to maintain a relatively stress-free lifestyle can affect your baby's overall health, intelligence and creative talents when they are older.

Of course, it's not always possible to avoid stress when your baby is on the way. Aside from anxieties about the health of your unborn baby and concerns about the birth and coping with the responsibility of looking after a new baby, expectant mothers often find themselves anxious about taking maternity leave or involved in stressful house moves or renovations as they try to make room for the new member of the family. However, the science suggests it's important that we do all we can to maintain calmer lifestyles during pregnancy.

In May 2007, research carried out by Professor Vivette Glover at Imperial College London and the consultant obstetrician Pampa Sarkar from Wexham Park Hospital, Berkshire, found that cortisol, the stress hormone which causes tiredness and depression in the long term, can be measured in the amniotic fluid around an unborn child as early as 17 weeks into the pregnancy of stressed mums-to-be. It seems that when mothers-to-be are anxious, the feeling passes physically to their baby, and the effects of long-term sustained stress do affect your baby's brain development.

Findings by Professor Vivette Glover found that babies of mothers who had sustained high levels of cortisol during pregnancy had an IQ ten points below average as well as higher anxiety levels and attention deficit problems. In terms of creative abilities, it is known that children who are anxious and who have short attention spans are less likely to be creative or to engage in imaginative play.

It's important to reduce your stress levels as far as possible. Here are some ways to do this:

Seek support
When you need to take some time out for yourself let family and friends know how they can help you to prepare for the new baby. Accept offers of help after the birth, such as help with cooking and laundry, so there will be less pressure on you in the first few weeks of motherhood.

Take regular rests
Try to wind down once a day. Studies show that ill effects tend to come from long bouts of sustained stress, so taking just short periods of time to relax regularly can have hugely beneficial effects for you and your baby even if you can't remove the stress entirely.

Know your rights
Under UK law you are entitled to the right to a reasonable amount of paid time off for antenatal appointments. What is considered 'reasonable' is not defined in law, however, the employer has to have a good reason for not giving permission. You are also entitled to special health and safety protection. For example, you should be protected from lifting or handling heavy loads, standing or sitting for long periods of time, or working long hours.

Meditate
There are wide-ranging studies revealing how beneficial meditation is for you and your baby during pregnancy. As well as reducing

anxiety, insomnia and depression, studies have revealed it can reduce blood pressure and heart rate. Psychologists Michael Murphy and Steven Donovan of the Esalen Institute have also reported that meditation has a wide range of benefits for your child's emotional and psychological development, enhancing perceptual ability, concentration, empathy and overall creativity.

Insight

Yoga is often combined with meditation during pregnancy as a way of combining the benefits of meditation with the physical benefits of relaxation and breathing exercises. However, be sure to get proper advice from a prenatal yoga expert and check with your doctor whether it is safe for you to do this.

Talk to your baby

Studies by Dr Anthony DeCasper of the University of North Carolina, reveal that from around the third trimester, your baby can tell his or her mother's voice apart from anyone else's, and that it often calms the baby's heart rate. Talking to your baby also helps you to bond with your 'bump' and release the 'love' hormone oxytocin, helping your baby to associate your calming tones with feelings of well-being and emotional security.

Listen to music

One common perception is that classical music can help your baby to become more intelligent and creative. Although there is much debate over whether this is true, a study published in 2008 by Professor Chung-Hey Chen, who led the study at Kaohsiung Medical University in Taiwan, found that pregnant women who listened to a CD of classical and new age music every day for two weeks were less anxious, stressed and depressed by the end of the study. Whether you switch to classical music in the car, or listen to it before bedtime, it can reduce your stress levels. From around 30 weeks, your baby's hearing and cognitive skills will allow him or her to listen in too.

However, it's a popular myth, fuelled by dozens of products available for new parents, that playing classical music to your baby can fuel their intelligence and cognitive abilities.

The truth is, although there are many benefits to playing all kinds of music to your baby during pregnancy, there's no evidence at all to support this theory about classical music.

The myth has come about largely from a study carried out about 60 years ago in which factory workers were found to have increased spatial-temporal task performance when they listened to Mozart piped into the factory floor. Spatial-temporal ability is the ability to visualize spatial patterns and mentally manipulate them over a time-ordered sequence of spatial transformations. In fact the research showed that this 'Mozart effect' was not only limited to this one specific area of intelligence, but that it was temporary.

However, other research does still point to the fact that music played to unborn children can help their development after 30 weeks, when most experts agree that babies can recognize patterns that make up music.

Studies such as those carried out by Dr Alexandra Lamont of Leicester University and Dr Roberta Polverini-Rey at the California School of Professional Psychology, reveal that babies remember and are soothed by this music up to a year after their birth, even if the music is loud and fast. The fact that babies remember and show reaction to this music suggests 'increased levels of cognitive development' resulting from *in utero* exposure to music.

Studies also reveal that newborn babies have surprising musical intelligence too. When you sing the lullaby that you sang to your child before birth, ensure that it is in the same tempo and key. It seems that babies can tell the difference and do not show a preference for the same songs if the key is slightly higher than the version they have heard once or twice a week in the womb.

In terms of preparing your child for a life enhanced by their intuitive inventiveness and imagination, you simply need to make sure the music you choose is music which you love too. The feeling of well-being, calm and enjoyment you gain from listening to it, will help your baby connect the music to the same pleasurable feelings when they are born. This not only gives them a way to express and share emotions before they have developed enough to do that verbally, but you are also helping to instil a deep-seated love of music and understanding of the way it can enrich your day-to-day life.

Preparing the nursery

Most parents put a good deal of time and care into preparing a baby's new nursery, and with good reason. The room where your baby sleeps will have a marked influence on how they behave. Here are a few tips to make your child's nursery one that promotes well-being and enhances their natural creativity and playfulness.

CHOOSING COLOURS

Studies dating back to those of Dr L.B. Wexner in 1954 have established clear links between colour and mood, but collective research suggests that the general temperature of colours, i.e. warmer or cooler, has as much influence as the overall shade. For this reason, it is important to think about how the natural light of the room will affect the particular shades of the colour you choose. Whites and blues are known to be calming and soothing, but in a darker room they can be cold and depressing. If your child's room is filled with natural light, however, then the colours are ideal. In slightly darker rooms, creams and pale yellows or slightly warmer neutral shades will provide a backdrop that's calming yet less stark and will help your baby to sleep more easily. If you're sceptical about the impact bright colours have on mood and behaviour, bear in mind that there's solid research to back this up.

A series of studies carried out by the Department of Education in Connecticut (1961) found that in schools where colour changes were made, students showed a marked decrease in behavioural problems. A more recent study in 2004 by Dr Naz Kaya and

Dr Helen Epps at the University of Georgia was yet another in a long line of studies to reveal strong emotional responses to different colours.

Dr Max Luscher, a psychologist who devised the Luscher colour test in 1969, even claimed that colours induce physical responses, for example red increases blood pressure and respiratory rate. His work, and that of the many other environmental psychologists who have found links between colours and mood, have been used throughout the advertising and commercial world for decades now. Fast food restaurants for example, use vivid red to make sure customers eat faster and stay in the premises for shorter periods.

This is not to say children should not be exposed to bright colours. Children do love colour, and it stimulates their creative imagination. But too many bright colours, such as red, orange and yellow are very stimulating and this can be a problem in a nursery for young babies who can so easily be over-stimulated by their new environment.

Top tip
One way to strike a balance is to scatter a few toys, cushions or throws in bold shades, or to paint the skirting boards and lintels in bright colours to add more interesting shades to the room.

How colour affects mood
The effects of colour vary depending on individual personality, but below is a guide to the most common emotional responses related to different shades:

- **Blues:** *calming and restful*
- **Whites:** *ambiguous responses. Some researchers have found white to be associated with calm and hope, others have found it is linked to negative emotions and depression*
- **Creams:** *calming and restful*
- **Yellows:** *happiness and creativity*

- ▶ **Oranges:** *excitement*
- ▶ **Reds:** *passion, excitement*
- ▶ **Greens:** *restful and strongly associated with peacefulness, nature and imagination*
- ▶ **Purples:** *deeper shades are associated with depression*
- ▶ **Black:** *anger and fear*
- ▶ **Browns and neutrals:** *sadness*
- ▶ **Pink:** *paler pinks are calming and can warm a room, brighter pinks are associated with excitement and some studies reveal it has a slightly tranquillizing effect.*

Insight

Children can associate different emotions to colour better than adults. The shade of the colour is very important. A study at the University of California found that preschool children associate bright colours with positive feelings and negative feelings to darker shades.

LIGHTING

Lighting needs to be soft. Try to avoid having lights that shine down from the ceiling into your baby's eyes at night. Up-lighters, wall lights or shaded lamps creating soft pools of light can help your child to feel more peaceful and can lighten up the room enough for play on a grey day. Moving lanterns that slide patterns across the walls and ceilings can be wonderful mood setters, but avoid playing them just before bedtime as they can be a bit over-stimulating for some babies.

SOUNDS

Many parents forget to use all five senses when planning a room. This is important because while we tend to focus on colours and decor, the visual sense is relatively alien to a newborn child. So far in their lives, sound has been the main connection to the outside world, and through sound, you can help to make their environment more familiar and calming.

Have a sound system so you can play music at different times of the day for your child. When babies are born, their sleep cycles are very short, and babies need to gradually adjust to the normal 24-hour sleep and wake cycle of the outside world. Playing soothing music or singing lullabies before bedtime, and playing more lively music in the morning as they are being dressed can reinforce this cycle and help them to adjust. As they do, they will begin to sleep less during the day and for longer through the night.

Hanging softly musical chimes is another idea to add gentle stimulation to their room.

THINGS TO TOUCH

From an early age your baby will be learning a good deal through his or her sense of touch, and providing different fabrics and textures in their room will help them to develop this sense and give them more to explore than simply what they see and hear. Fluffy cushions, shiny smooth toys and touch-and-feel books, or perhaps a frieze on the wall decorated with differently textured materials all add an extra dimension to the room and will stimulate your baby's curiosity and imagination.

ART

Choosing a few intriguing or simply beautiful pictures for the wall will help your baby to understand the value of art from a very early age. You could buy postcards and frame them against white card in clip frames, or even ask an older sibling to paint some pictures and hang them up in picture frames painted to match the room.

SHAPES AND ANIMALS

Babies are drawn to geometric shapes and animals, and constant
exposure to these things can help to develop cognitive and language
skills. Try to find a place for them in the nursery, for example in a
mobile or frieze, or in the patterns on curtains or throws.

Birth to three months

From the moment your baby is born, his or her brain is developing
thousands of connections between brain cells. These connections
enable us to think, and the process of building those connections
is what happens as we learn. Even before birth your baby will be
listening to you and the world around them. Their sense of sight is
less well developed at this stage. This is due to the fact that the area of
the brain which controls vision is still developing, and it will take an
average of eight months before your baby can see (almost) as well as
an adult. The sense of touch is immensely important, although for the
first few weeks your baby won't even realize their hands are part of
them. Many of the things you can do to help your child begin to start
learning and understanding, parents do instinctively. Holding your
baby and gazing into his or her eyes from about 20 centimetres as
you sing, talk and laugh helps them to develop many early skills. It is
also important to nurture their sense of security and routine and not
to over-stimulate them. Make use of the brief wakeful times between
feeding and sleeping to communicate and play with your baby. As the
weeks go by, this time will increase at your baby's own unique pace.

Here are some games and toys that will help to cultivate your
baby's imagination from these very early stages.

THINGS TO DO WITH BOOKS

Act out a story
Find a short story which involves a few different animals. When your baby is awake, act out the story, doing all the voices and noises, and adding plenty of smiles and laughter in between. Your newborn will learn a lot from you talking animatedly to him or her, and will begin to understand the meaning of different facial expressions if you make them clear in the story. You're also introducing your baby early to the rhythm and fun of storytelling, and that can never begin too early if you want to encourage a wild imagination.

Make some finger puppets
Buy or make some brightly coloured finger puppets and use them to act out a story. From an early age you are introducing books as something fun and this is also a way for you to interact while introducing colourful and textured objects. You can also help your baby's tracking movements by moving the puppets from side to side gradually so they follow and help them to begin to understand about their own hands.

THINGS TO DO WITH MUSIC

Have a daily singing session
Young babies love rhythm and can already recognize patterns of music. Have a daily singing session if you can, roughly at the same time every day, of the same four or five songs they seem to react to the most (you may find these are songs or pieces of music you sang or played to them in the womb). The repetition will help them

to learn and the routine will help them to feel secure. You're also helping them to associate music with a sense of belonging, ritual and good feelings.

Insight

Baby signing can be a good way to help your child to communicate and understand before they are able to talk. Many baby signing methods involve teaching signs during songs. For more information visit www.singandsign.com or www.babysign.co.uk.

Dance with your baby

From birth, babies love rhythm and being held by you. Having a daily dance with them around the living room (singing is optional!) is a good way to help them develop and enjoy that sense of rhythm, and again associates music with fun and good feelings. Your baby is also learning a tremendous amount about patterns of sounds.

GAMES TO PLAY

Make up some tickling games

You might like to stick to some old favourites like, 'This little Piggy went to market' or 'Round and round the garden, goes the teddy bear' where you make a few steps with your fingers up the baby's arms or legs then tickle them on their tummies. You're giving them a really basic understanding of narrative and helping them to be aware of their bodies – as well as having a lot of fun, which is the best part.

Spin the mirror game

Unbreakable mirrors are a useful toy for young babies of this age as they are beginning to respond to faces. Have a child-safe mirror in the nursery and spin it around so your child's face appears and disappears. This is a good way to introduce the game of peek-a-boo, especially to very anxious babies, because in this game, the adult who is playing the game does not disappear. The game is also a problem-solving exercise for your child. His or her curiosity will be awakened as they wonder where the face goes and why it reappears.

Make a texture box
You can buy touch-and-feel books of course, but you might like
to make up a box of seven or eight different textures, for example
feathers, a wooden spoon, a patch of fleece, a square of silk, some
shiny cellophane or a piece of bark or wood. When you take out
the box, you can give them to your baby to examine and play with
one at a time.

THINGS TO DO WITH COLOUR

Use colours to reinforce your daily routine
In our adult lives we naturally use decor and colour to set moods
and tone for events such as mealtimes or parties. You can also
use it to reinforce a sense of routine for your child and to make
sure colour is a part of your child's daily world. For example, set
down a rainbow throw on your chair at story time, or set out a
bright blue cloth over the feeding chair or over your shoulders at
mealtimes to signal with colour that it's time to eat.

Three to six months

By this stage, your baby will probably be enormously curious
about the world around them. They'll probably have favourite
toys, but enjoy looking at new things. At this age they'll probably
prefer to sit in a chair or be propped up with cushions so they can
see what's going on. They'll also probably be laughing now and
be experimenting by making lots of different noises on their own.
Here are some toys and games to encourage your baby's natural
sense of curiosity and playfulness at this stage.

GAMES TO PLAY

Play copycat
Your baby was born with the instinct to imitate you, and will
probably find it enormously funny if you do the same now. When
your baby is making new sounds, get close and copy them. It will

encourage them to try all kinds of new noises and eventually they'll begin to play back, copying you.

Water games
Your baby will probably love splashing around in the water at this stage. One thing that fascinates children is simply watching water being poured in the light. The way water moves and feels, separates, and forms bubbles and ripples can be endlessly fascinating to your baby. Get some clear plastic bowls and measuring jugs and play with them during bath time, pouring the water from up high and dripping it onto arms or legs. Help your baby to look at and feel water in lots of different ways.

Have a funny face competition
See how many strange faces you can pull and get your baby to copy you. Try gurning, wiggling your ears and tongue, blowing raspberries. It helps your baby to practise moving different facial muscles, and also to interact in games and play.

THINGS TO DO WITH MUSIC

Musical bubbles
Babies of this age are fascinated by the colours and magic of bubbles. Surround them with bubbles and play some classical or bouncy music. This can create a real sense of magic and wonder for your baby.

Make a baby orchestra
If you have a baby gym, hang some wind chimes, rattles and bells over the bar, so your baby can experiment by using their body to knock the toys and enjoy the sounds they make.

Play musical toys
Have a box with four or five of your baby's favourite toys inside and play some music. When it stops you reach in, and pull out one of the toys, and give it to your baby to hold and play with for a minute until you repeat the process. You bring a little music, fun and magic into the day and add a bit of creative imagination to the normal business of play.

How to involve older siblings

The arrival of a new baby is often upsetting for an older sibling, who ends up feeling left out and jealous at the attention you have to give to a younger baby. It's not always easy or possible, but as well as the tried and trusted method of asking your child to help you look after your baby and marking out a space of time each day for one-to-one time with the older child, try to encourage older siblings to get more involved in playing with the baby by asking them to help make and invent new games and entertainment for the new arrival.

Your older sibling can help you make things such as the texture box, or put together a box for musical toys. As well as getting them usefully involved, it also encourages your older child to think creatively with regard to what entertainment and toys they can dream up for the baby, with the added bonus of bringing the two of them closer through play.

Here are some suggestions:

▶ *Ask the older sibling to put together a little zoo of furry animals they can introduce to the baby, describing the animals and making the noises for them.*
▶ *Suggest your older child makes up a new tickling rhyme.*
▶ *Sing 'I can sing a rainbow' to the baby and ask your older child if they could pick out things of each colour in the song so they can show them to the baby as you sing the words.*
▶ *Take the children to the library and ask your older child to pick out four or five books that he or she thinks would be right for the baby as well as choosing their own books.*
▶ *Suggest your older child sets up a tea party and invite the baby along as a guest. You can hold the baby as the older sibling picks out pretend food and pours pretend drinks for him or her. It's a good way to encourage your older sibling to think about the needs of the new baby.*
▶ *Have a little frame hanging near the cot in the nursery and ask your older child to draw or make a different picture for their new brother or sister each week.*

10 THINGS TO REMEMBER

1 *Eating foods rich in folic acid, omega 3 oils and choline can help your baby's brain development and affect your child's long-term learning abilities.*

2 *Avoiding stress during pregnancy may help to reduce your child's anxiety and improve their health and natural creativity.*

3 *Unborn children can hear and respond to music. It may even help them to become faster learners later in childhood.*

4 *The colours you choose for your baby's nursery can affect their mood.*

5 *Think about the sounds, textures and smells in the nursery as well as its visual appearance.*

6 *Young babies cannot see as well as adults and will take around eight months before their vision is developed to a similar level to that of adults.*

7 *The best time for creative play is in the brief time during your baby's routine when he or she is not tired, hungry or uncomfortable.*

8 *Give your baby lots of safe things to touch, and explore with their mouth, as this sense is key in development at this stage.*

9 *Colour and music can help you to communicate everything from what time of day it is to different emotions at this age.*

10 *Involve older siblings in games with the baby.*

5

Six months to one year

In this chapter you will learn:
- *how encouraging creativity can help your child to develop at this age*
- *the golden rules for encouraging creativity at this age*
- *activities and games which will enhance their natural curiosity and imagination.*

If the birth and adjusting to life with a newborn has felt like a roller coaster, prepare for another period of very marked change in your baby. This key stage of six months to one year is the phase when most babies learn to walk and talk. Although not all children will have said their first words or taken their first steps by their first birthday, they will be well on their way.

As your child begins to develop these motor and language skills, they will begin to express their personality. Self-expression and the ability to come up with new thoughts and ideas are becoming more and more important to your child, which is why children are more creative at this age than at almost any other. Your son might not be able to convey his anger in words, but he will be able to bang ferociously on the table if he is feeling frustrated. And while your daughter might not be able to tell you she's lost her toy, with a little imagination and problem solving she'll be able to use her body language and sounds to let you know something's wrong.

During this phase, your child's brain is developing at a tremendous rate as they begin to form the neural connections which enable language skills, locomotion and communication and social skills. In this chapter we'll explore imaginative ways to encourage and facilitate creative development.

Golden rules

GIVE ANIMATED PRAISE

When your child tries something new or solves a problem, be really animated and attentive in your praise. Children of this age respond well to encouraging noises and facial expressions. Clap, cheer and show lots of interest, especially when they are trying new things, or have found a way to do something differently all by themselves.

UNDERSTAND THAT BAD BEHAVIOUR IS UNINTENTIONAL

Children of this age certainly behave badly sometimes, but they do not yet have the empathetic or social skills to understand why what they are doing is 'wrong'. Crucially at this stage, babies are learning about cause and effect. Your child may have understood that throwing porridge over you in the morning makes you upset, but they don't yet understand that it's wrong to do this.

It is difficult not to react with distress or anger when babies repeatedly do disruptive things. However, part of their development stage means that they are fascinated by their new ability to cause the same thing to happen over and over again. When this happens, they begin to make connections and understand that what is happening is linked to their actions and not simply a random coincidence.

Of course, you can't be expected to remain calm every time your child throws his food on the floor, but do be aware that every time you shout or display stress because they have tried something new, you influence their attitudes to experimenting in the future.

Most babies are fairly resilient to this and will, in fact, want to see mummy shouting again, but more anxious children might begin to shy away from trying new things altogether.

Insight

Before the age of one, babies do not have very long-term memories, and so even if you manage to convey one day that you do not like a certain kind of behaviour, they will have forgotten all about it tomorrow. Your best tactic at this age is distraction.

Sarah, mum to James, two

'My son James was very naughty at this age. He used to try to climb behind the television and play with the wires, or he'd deliberately tip his breakfast over his sister and laugh. I didn't realize I was shouting at him so much until my own grandmother came to visit. She pointed out in a very non-judgemental way that I was shouting when he even went near one of his 'danger' zones and suggested he seemed to be becoming a little more timid. I realized that I was actually discouraging him from exploring and trying out new things. I've tried to be a lot calmer in my tone of voice and a lot more hesitant to shout at him to stop what he's doing now. I won't tolerate him doing things that cause damage, or hurt others or himself, but I hold back a little before I intervene.'

The best way to try to discourage inappropriate experimentation is to repeat the word 'No' firmly but calmly when they carry out the behaviour and give them another toy or activity to distract their attention, or simply move them away from the situation.

BE CREATIVE YOURSELF

One of the key ways babies of this age are learning is by watching you. If you take pleasure from drawing your own pictures, or regularly play a musical instrument, your children will begin to understand from an early age how creative activities can bring enjoyment for their own sake.

LOOK FOR CREATIVITY IN UNUSUAL PLACES

Every child is unique and although finger paints and play dough might be popular ways for them to play and express their imagination now, do remember there are hundreds of ways your child might be expressing their individual creative style. For example, your child might like to line up their toys in a neat line, or wiggle their toes and feet in time to the car stereo. Other children might enjoy doing the same puzzle over and over again, or spend hours working out how to move cushions and toys to build platforms to reach new things. Every time your child recognizes and solves a problem, try to identify the ways in which your child expresses their creativity and be imaginative about ways to encourage them.

Insight

During this year your child will become increasingly mobile. The ways they discover to move from A to B, be it bottom shuffling, crawling or rolling, are a fascinating display of their resourcefulness and creative thinking.

Games, toys and activities to play with your baby

Here are some suggestions of fun activities that encourage creative development at this age. Of course, children of this age must always be supervised during these activities.

Remember: Children develop at very different paces at this age. For this reason, it's a good idea to look in the sections after this one and choose the activities and games which are most appropriate for your child.

THINGS TO MAKE FOR YOUR BABY

Edible finger paints
Your baby will love the feeling of the paint oozing through his or her fingers.

You will need:

- ▶ 225 g/8 oz corn starch
- ▶ 6 tbsp sugar
- ▶ 1 tsp salt
- ▶ 1 litre/2 pints of cold water
- ▶ Additive-free food colourings.

Mix the corn starch into a smooth paste in a saucepan, then gradually add water, sugar and salt. Heat on a low heat for 10 minutes or so until the mixture thickens to the right gloopy consistency. Remove the pan from the heat and pour it into as many little pots or pallets as you want colours (old play dough pots are good). When it's cool add a few drops of colouring into each pot as desired.

Play dough
Babies love the feel and texture of dough at this age, but they also love eating it. The solution is edible play dough. This recipe is non-toxic to young children in small amounts, although of course they do need to be supervised and the dough must be kept out of reach at other times.

You will need:

- ▶ 300 g/9.5 oz flour
- ▶ 400 g/14 oz salt
- ▶ 6 tsp cream of tarter
- ▶ 3 tbsp cooking oil
- ▶ 1.5 pints of water.

Dissolve the salt in the water. Put the dry ingredients into a pan and gradually add the water to make a smooth paste. Stir constantly over medium heat until the mixture can be formed into a ball. Knead the dough mixture for 1 or 2 minutes until the texture matches that of play dough. Add natural food colouring as required.

Bubble mixture
Children love bubbles, and from this one simple activity they have their very first science lesson as well as experiencing interesting shapes, colours and textures.

Mix together:

▶ *½ a pint of water*
▶ *2 tbsp of glycerine (available from pharmacies)*
▶ *2 tbsp of baby shampoo or wash.*

THINGS TO DO WITH MUSIC

Make up a story using nursery rhymes
Children of this age love the repetition, rhythm and melody of nursery rhymes, and they also love hearing you tell stories. They might not understand everything, but they love watching your expressions and hearing your voice and as the weeks pass they will come to understand more and more language, even though they're not able to speak yet. Combining stories with music makes the nursery rhymes more fun and encourages your child to think about the meaning of the songs.

Make up your own story using four or five favourite nursery rhymes. For example, a little girl wishes she could learn to fly and she wishes on a star (*Twinkle Twinkle Little Star*), and then a little elf appears and they slide down a beautiful rainbow together (*I Can Sing a Rainbow*). Or, you can weave songs into your child's favourite stories. Keep the stories short and limit the number of songs to four or five, as children don't have a long attention span.

Old MacDonald's Farm with pictures
Draw or cut out pictures of five or six interesting animals on some card and write the name of the animal under each one, then cut them into equal cards and place them on the floor. Then, singing *Old MacDonald's Farm*, ask your child to point to the animal which they want to come next in the song. Encourage them to name the animal and/or make the noise. As time goes by, they'll

begin to recognize the names, pictures and noises. They'll also begin to understand about making choices.

Make a car karaoke CD

For long or regular journeys, it's a good idea to make up a CD of your child's favourite songs. It could be anything from Beethoven to the latest top ten hits to tunes from musicals like *Mary Poppins* or *Chitty Chitty Bang Bang*. Play your child a variety of different types of music, and gradually build up a list of ten or more tracks they really love. You may find that their preferences change and they love to hear the same song repeated over and over again.

> **Insight**
>
> If older siblings are involved, car karaoke can dissolve into furious arguments. To defuse in-car rows, try asking the older child to pick out songs that the whole family will like.

Make a baby orchestra

Your baby will love discovering how to make noises at this age, not just with his or her voice, but by banging and clanging and squeezing whatever they can get their hands on. It's always fun to make a drum kit using saucepans and wooden spoons, but raid the rest of the household to make a versatile baby orchestra for your baby to experiment with on a rainy afternoon. Hang spoons from bits of string, use old paintbrushes as drum beaters and find large bits of tissue or newspaper to rip and scrunch.

THINGS TO DO IN THE LIVING ROOM

Create a baby treasure trail

Your baby is learning to move him or herself around at the moment and one of the key things that will motivate them is curiosity. Your baby is also beginning to understand that objects exist even when they can't see them. Using cushions, throws and sheets, hide several favourite toys or 'treasures' (such as crumpled pieces of tissue paper, bells or a furry material) and encourage your baby to crawl, bottom shuffle or cruise along to each new discovery.

Play the cuddle monster

Two key things your baby is learning about at this age are showing affection and humour, and you can use these to introduce imaginative play in this game. When you and your baby are playing, make a show of going behind the sofa or a cushion and then jumping out as the cuddle monster and giving them a big tickle and a hug. As your child's motor skills develop and they begin to crawl and cruise you can begin to have cuddle monster chases.

Make a tissue tunnel

If your baby is learning to crawl, this game will encourage them to develop their locomotion skills and also enables them to play with colour, sound and texture. Using sticky tape, secure different sheets of tissue paper to the area behind the sofa, a play tunnel, chairs or other sturdy furniture. Then encourage your baby to move through it, ripping and scrunching the tissue as they go.

Take your child for a horsey ride

By six months your child should just about be starting to sit up, and in the months which follow he or she may be able to sit independently on ride-on toys and move along. It is at this point where you may feel it is safe to start playing make believe and giving him or her some 'horsey' rides on your back through the living room. You could pretend they are a cowboy, sing 'Horsey, horsey don't you stop', or pretend to be a pet elephant or a pet bear. As well as developing physical skills and balance, this game encourages make-believe play.

THINGS TO DO WITH FOOD

Make a food rainbow

Your baby will be starting with soft foods and progressing to finger foods during this period. One thing you can do for a fun mealtime is to purée, or later soften, brightly coloured natural foods such as peppers, tomatoes, cucumbers and mangoes to make up a food rainbow in little pots.

Ask your child which colours he or she likes first, naming the colours, then ask them which foods they like when they've tasted each one.

They'll love the bright colours, be tempted to try new foods and above all they'll love mixing them up and making a (very creative) mess.

> ### Insight
> Many parents do not like children to play with food at the dinner table, but this is a good age to help your child to associate food with fun before your baby can really understand and remember lessons about table manners and before they can handle utensils well.

Play the smelly game

Pick four or five things with a strong scent, such as a rose, a lemon, some cinnamon, a pine cone and maybe a gingerbread man to finish. Rub each scent onto small, separate pieces of blank paper (use scented oils or spices if it's easier) and place each item representing the scent on the table. Now your child has to smell the different pieces of paper and guess which item has the same smell. Children love guessing games at this age, and this adds the extra element of using and exploring their sense of smell.

Make some animal biscuits

Your child may be too young to take a very active part in baking, but he or she will enjoy attempting to mix as well as experiencing the textures and scents and watching you create something with basic ingredients. You can add interest by asking them to choose which animal shapes they would like you to cut out from the dough.

VANILLA BISCUITS
You will need:

- ▶ 225 g/8 oz of sugar
- ▶ 130 g/4.5 oz butter
- ▶ 1 tsp vanilla essence
- ▶ 1 egg
- ▶ 225 g/8 oz self-raising flour.

In a mixing bowl cream together the sugar, butter and vanilla essence. Then add one egg and mix. Then add the flour and make into a soft dough. Finally, flatten and cut out your animal shapes. Bake at 190°C for 15–20 minutes.

THINGS TO DO OUTSIDE

Go on a garden nature trail

On the left-hand side of a page, draw five or six things your child might find in the garden: a leaf, a snail, a flower, a tree, etc. Then, carrying your child, or as they crawl or cruise, go around the garden with them looking to see if they can find each thing. When you do, put a big bright sticker, tick, or gold star by each one before you look for the next one. As well as helping with language, this helps your baby to relate pictures to the real world and encourages them to look for new things in the garden. If you regularly go for walks in the woods or by a river, you can make your own nature trail based on animals and plants you know you're likely to see.

Make a season table

As your baby gets a little older, they will start to understand the passing of time and the world changing around them. You can encourage this by creating a season shelf, table or corner and helping your child to collect things for it. For example, you could include leaves, pictures of trees with golden branches, wellington boots and fallen nuts or pine cones on an autumn display, or flowers, pictures of birds nests, and buds or blossom for spring. Make a point of changing the season table once the next season is officially underway and make it a ritual you do together.

Make sand pictures

If you don't have access to a sand pit, you can buy some play sand and pour it into a plastic tray. Then spend some time drawing swirls and pictures in the sand. Let your baby watch you making swirls, dolphins or boats in the sand, and let them have a go in their own time. They'll enjoy making the shapes but also the texture and feel of the sand through their fingers. Don't give them any other toys to play with such as buckets and spades at this point. The key to inspiring creativity and to encouraging them to come up with new ways of doing things, is to give them fewer props. There is so much your child can do and enjoy at this age with just sand and his or her hands.

Make a rainbow water play
Using a water play tray or just clear Tupperware boxes, place a few pots of water around for your child to play with and add a few drops of food colouring to each container so you have lots of different colours. Let your child practise splashing, and mixing the colours and pouring.

Make a safe corner in the garden
At this age your child will be rapidly discovering the big wide world around them and will be loving playing outside when weather permits. However, most gardens contain numerous hazards for young children. Secure a specific area which is theirs and fill it with things to provide scents, sounds and natural things to play with for safe fun. You can use temporary barriers by erecting a windbreaker or low-level trellis on a corner of the lawn. Ensure you cater for all your baby's senses. For example, you could put rain-catching bells in the corner, or hang wind chimes from overhanging branches. You might also want to install a child-safe water feature or colourful windmills.

Top tip
Babies have thin skin and underdeveloped melanin, causing their skin to burn more quickly than that of older children. If your child is outside between the hours of 10 a.m. and 4 p.m., even on a cloudy day, make sure they are covered in clothing or wearing sunscreen specially designed for their age group. Parents of children under the age of six months are often advised not to apply sunscreen but to cover children in hats, and light clothing on hot days. If in doubt, ask your local pharmacist.

For a list of child-friendly plants and shrubs and other garden features, the following websites may be helpful: www.thekidsgarden.co.uk and www.safegardening.co.uk. The garden safety checklist at the Royal Society for the Prevention of Accidents website is also helpful, visit www.rospa.com.

Insight

If you don't have a garden, why don't you take a windbreak to a corner of your local park on a warm afternoon. You could also grow pot plants and window boxes in any outdoor space you have, so your child can enjoy watching things grow, and discover the textures and smells of different herbs and flowers.

THINGS TO DO WITH BOOKS

Set up a story corner

Books and stories are especially important to your baby at this stage, helping them to learn about the world, people's emotions and discovering the meaning of new concepts through the context of stories. So, encourage them to enjoy looking at books alone and with you by making a comfortable, accessible story corner in your home. Make sure the books face out on the shelf, or are kept in baskets which your child can access easily. Put colourful rugs, cushions and dolls or toys they might find in the stories around the area. Also, make sure it's not somewhere people will be walking back and forth throughout the day, or where they'll be disturbed by noise from the television or washing machine. As well as encouraging your child to read, you are also giving them somewhere they can enjoy being alone which is invaluable to fostering their creativity.

Make a baby obstacle course with a story

Using a favourite story, plan a little obstacle course around the living room that goes with it. You can use pillows for mountains, tissues or scarves for rivers and chairs covered in sheets for tunnels. The obstacles not only add interest, but help your child to understand some of the words more clearly.

Make shape puppets for stories

Help your child to learn about shapes by making some finger puppets of geometric shapes to play the parts in stories. Your child will understand the difference between a triangle and a circle far more quickly if they are characters in stories.

Pin new words on the walls

It's during this phase that some children begin to say their first words. A good way to encourage them and to gradually introduce the connection between words in written and spoken form is to display the new word they have learned most recently and by writing it in big, colourful letters and pinning it to a wall or noticeboard.

Role play with dolls or teddies

Your child will be beginning to love stories now, but they will have a short attention span and may not listen to a longer story all the way through. Add a little spice to the entertainment by using a red tea towel to make a dolly Little Red Riding Hood.

THINGS TO DO WITH TOYS

Make magic brick castles in the night

Before you go to bed, every so often, creep into your child's room and create a beautiful and magical surprise for them in the night. You could build a castle from building blocks, or put a new dress on a doll. Then you can act surprised in the morning and wonder if perhaps the elves or fairies have visited.

Make up a baby bag

As your baby develops motor skills of picking things up and moving them around, and also begins to understand that objects exist when they can't see them, one toy that they will love is a baby bag. Get them their own box or soft cloth bag and play a game where you fill it with different intriguing objects. It could be their favourite soft toy, feathers, scrunched up tissue paper, pictures of animals, squeaky toys that make noise. They'll love the sense of mystery and discovery. Once they've taken each thing out and looked at it, let them spend time playing with the things which intrigue them most. As the standards set out in the Early Years Foundation Stage outline, children learn better when they are playing with things they have chosen and which they are enjoying.

Give teddy his own story

As your child begins to love stories and develops a preference for a favourite toy, build up a special story for the toy. If you start at this age, as your child is beginning to develop longer-term memories, it will hold much more magic for them. For example, you could make up the story that a favoured teddy bear is a teddy explorer who came all the way from the mountains, or pretend that your daughter's favourite doll was made by the fairies just for her. When you make up stories, this encourages your child to use and express their own imagination.

Alter the toy display each week

According to the guidelines set out in the Early Years Foundation Stage standards for child carers in the UK, creativity is encouraged if children can initiate their own play from a variety of appropriate resources and activities. You can stimulate your child's interest and encourage them to think differently about the toys they have if you alter the way they are displayed and rotate different toys for their attention. For example, you might want to select different toys each week to place in the bedroom window, or on a shelf or bedside table.

Top tip

You can use the toys to give your child new ideas for play too. For example, you could set out a teddy bear building a brick tower, or a doll drawing a rainbow with crayons, or put a book about mermaids in a make-believe sea of blue and green tissue paper.

10 THINGS TO REMEMBER

1 Give lots of praise when your child tries to solve a problem on their own, even if the 'solution' doesn't quite work out.

2 Think before you say 'No' or 'Stop'. Children of this age hear that word so much. If what they are doing isn't harmful to themselves or property, can you avoid saying it, or even just take a deep breath and avoid displaying stress?

3 Be creative yourself. Sing, listen to music, and enjoy planning new fun games with your baby.

4 If you have time, try home-made recipes for things such as finger paints, play dough and bubbles. It makes the fun of the activity last twice as long and cost much less.

5 Mix up traditional activities, such as singing nursery rhymes and reading stories, or putting unusual toys together.

6 Outdoor play sparks a lot of curiosity in your baby about the world around them, so try things like nature trails or season tables.

7 Choose books with really beautiful illustrations if you can. Even at this age, your child will relate to the colours and magic of lovely images. Understanding stories through pictures will help your child to learn more words.

8 Simple materials such as sand, flour or mud can keep your child happy for a long time as they explore the different textures and movement of them.

9 Babies develop at very different rates and this bears little relation to how clever, imaginative and skilled they will eventually become as adults.

10 Try to be aware of when your baby is over-stimulated and just needs quiet time and a cuddle.

6

One to two years

In this chapter you will learn:
- *how encouraging creativity can help your child to develop at this age*
- *the golden rules for encouraging creativity at this age*
- *activities and games which will enhance their natural curiosity and imagination.*

At this stage perhaps more than any other, children vary quite hugely in the rate at which they develop different abilities and skills. While some children will be walking by their first birthday or joining several words by 18 months, others take longer and perhaps develop different skills first. Generally speaking, however, before your child reaches his or her second birthday, they will begin to walk confidently and to put two words together. No matter how quickly they develop their language and locomotive skills, however, by the end of this momentous stage your toddler probably won't have enough language to fully communicate all the thoughts and feelings they are beginning to experience. Now, more than ever, it's important for them to develop creative ways to communicate their emotions.

For parents and carers, this is a particularly demanding stage, as children of this age need constant supervision. Newly discovered mobility and natural curiosity combine to make most toddlers almost magnetically drawn to dangerous situations. A natural inclination to explore with all five senses explains why many children of this age put new objects straight into their mouths.

Children's desire to enjoy and experiment with new textures also means that they often make a lot of mess, splashing with water for example, or smearing glue. But although this makes for chaotic craft activities, if you understand and anticipate this behaviour, you can plan activities which your child will thoroughly enjoy and learn a good deal from. Do bear in mind that at this age children are benefiting hugely from the creative process of experimenting with textures and ways to use the paintbrush. Creative products are rarely important to your child; it's the process that excites them.

Every child has a very different personality, and at this age your child will begin to express theirs more clearly. Most children begin to exhibit a preference for certain toys and activities during this year and this is often reflective of the ways in which they will express their creativity in later life. Although most children are instinctively very creative and imaginative at this age, this year you will have a huge influence on how confident your child is in expressing that creativity.

Golden rules

TALK, TALK, TALK

Your baby's vocabulary will expand tremendously this year, and the more you talk and describe the world around them, the faster they will learn. These new words and ideas will help to open up a whole new world for them, as they begin to understand colours, shapes, sizes, objects and animals. When talking to your child, you can speed up their linguistic development by being descriptive rather than simply repeating simple nouns. For example, rather than pointing to a bird in the tree and saying the word, point it out and say 'that bird is a beautiful, blue bird', or 'the lion in this book has a golden mane and a loud roar'.

> **Insight**
>
> As they start speaking, children are bound to get lots of
> words wrong (often in a really sweet way). Most language
> experts believe that we shouldn't correct our children, and
> that mistakes are part of the learning process. Instead, just
> say and use words correctly yourself, so they can learn in
> their own time.

GIVE LOTS OF PRAISE

Research such as that by Dr Kristen Kemple and Dr Gigi David
at the University of Florida reveal that self-esteem is linked very
strongly with how creative children are, and that children with
higher self-esteem tend to score more highly in tests of creativity.
You can help to build your child's confidence by giving regular,
genuine praise. Particularly pay attention to occasions when your
child dares to try something new.

DON'T BE PUSHY

In our competitive world where it is possible to look up the average
developmental milestones on the Internet, it can be difficult not to
be too expectant of our children. But remember, children's rates of
development begin to differ widely at this age. For example, the
average age for a child to be walking independently varies from as
young as 11 or 12 months to 18 months. Also, while some children
are talking in sentences by 18 months, the average age for a child
to combine two words for the first time is 19 months.

If you want to inspire a natural love of learning and
experimentation in your child, try to step back a little and follow
their lead. Children learn most quickly when they are playing
games and activities they have chosen themselves. If they are not
ready to sit through a long story, for example, or they simply can't
get to grips with simple puzzles, set out several different toys and
activities for them to choose from. Children instinctively gravitate
towards the play which is most beneficial for them.

It is also helpful to remember that the speed at which they develop in these early years has little bearing on how gifted or creative they will eventually become. Famously, Albert Einstein did not begin joining words together until well after his second birthday, prompting his parents to become concerned that he had learning disabilities.

> ### Insight
> It is important to be aware of the key milestones of average development so you can seek help if your child seems to be experiencing problems. Most children, for example, are expected to be crawling (or their version of it!) by 12 months, and to say some intelligible words before two years. If you're concerned, speak to your health visitor or doctor.

EXPLORE THE SENSES

At this age, your child will be extremely curious about using all five senses. Try to encourage this instinct rather than inhibiting it, by choosing activities which allow your child to make some mess, or experiment with taste, touch and smell so they can explore all their senses freely. Thinking of activities which allow them to explore different textures, sensations, scents and sounds will open up all kinds of creative avenues.

> ### Insight
> Your child instinctively uses all of her senses at this age to explore the world around her, in particular using touch and taste to explore new things. This is why babies of this age like to grab things and put them into their mouths.

GIVE YOUR CHILD FREE TIME

Many parents feel guilty about leaving their child to play alone for periods of time rather than sitting down with them to 'do something'. Yet the standards set out in the UK's Early Years Foundation Stage for nurseries and child carers specify that children need opportunities each day to spend at least 45 minutes to 1 hour engaging in uninterrupted, child-initiated play.

This is not to say you have no involvement. Children of this age need constant supervision, of course, and it is helpful to have an adult on hand to make suggestions to develop the play and to provide help should the child face some difficulty.

Top tip

It's easy to let day-to-day demands take up all your time. Pencil in at least half an hour of your day where you and your child don't actually have to do anything. Keep it sacred – don't fill it with chores or phone calls. Just enjoy the downtime and you'll teach your child to do the same.

Setting up a selection of activities and allowing your child to play without you hovering over them, however, allows them to explore and play in a way which really helps them to learn and develop in their own, unique way. This gives children the freedom and time they need to connect with their own thoughts and individual instincts, without outside interference.

REPETITION IS GOOD

You might not feel that your child is being particularly creative when they repeatedly scribble a few lines on a piece of paper then repeat the exercise several times, or when they build up three blocks of a tower then knock it down, over and over again. But children at this age learn a good deal from repetition. The child who knocks down his tower repeatedly is learning about cause and effect. Reading stories with lots of repeated phrases help children to grasp language and ideas.

Games, toys and activities to play with your developing baby

Here are some activities and ideas which can help to encourage creativity at this crucial phase in your child's development.

Remember: Children develop at very different paces at this age. For this reason, it's a good idea to look in the chapters before and after this one and to choose the activities and games which are most appropriate for your child. Children of this age must always be supervised during these activities.

WAYS TO ENCOURAGE MAKE-BELIEVE PLAY

Make a dressing-up box
Children of this age benefit from a dressing-up box because they are learning the fine motor skills involved in putting clothes on and taking them off and also beginning to play make-believe games. In order to make the dressing-up box one that will inspire imagination, steer clear of ready-made character costumes and stick to items such as hats, scarves, shoes and bags which can be adapted to a wide variety of different purposes. For example, a scarf can become a king's cloak or a flying carpet, a bag might be used for a pretend shopping trip or as a make-believe cauldron.

Copy me cleaning up
Set up a pretend living room for your child, using towels for rugs and cushions for tables and chairs, and explain you're going to play a cleaning up game. While you vacuum, your child copies and pretends to vacuum their room. When you dust, they can have a duster and dust too. You won't get many chores done before their attention wanders, but it's a way of involving them in your world and showing them how watching what others do can help them add new ideas into their own make-believe games.

Top tip
Try to include items for boys *and* girls in your selection of toys regardless of your child's gender. It's through our choices of toys and games that we can pass on stereotypes and deny our children the chance to experiment and play freely. Most boys of this age love trying on pretty shoes or walking around with handbags and equally many girls love playing cowboys and indians or pretending to be aliens or spacemen.

The magic sofa
Transform your sofa into a role-play area with the aid of a few simple props and introduce your toddler to a safe, make-believe zone. A plastic plate and a wooden spoon is all you need to turn the magic sofa into a car. Some carefully placed cushions and a vacuum cleaner nozzle and you have an aeroplane. By introducing some imaginary transformations to the sofa you'll encourage your child to initiate their own make-believe play.

THINGS TO DO IN THE LIVING ROOM

Play the opposites game
As your child begins to understand the world, he or she will begin to start thinking about how different objects and ideas relate to each other. A key part of this is understanding opposites. Draw four or five pairs of the same animal on separate pieces of card, and in each pair make the animals in some way opposite to each other. For example, draw a big dog and a small dog, a black dog and a white dog, a smiling dog and a sad dog. Pick out cards and ask your child to guess which card is the opposite.

Make a body chart
Using a roll of paper, draw the shape of a person, it can be a ballerina or a fireman or whatever your child loves. Then get some stickers or a brightly coloured pen and ask your child to mark where different body parts are on the picture. As well as teaching them about their bodies, it also helps them to understand that things can be real, or in pictures.

The touch and guess game
Get a drawstring bag or a solid container, with a hole big enough for your child to reach in and out of, and a collection of five or six things with contrasting textures. You could include a sponge, a furry toy, some wet play dough or a candle. Put them into the bag and ask your child to reach in and describe and guess what the item is.

THINGS TO DO WITH BOOKS

Tell some 'what happened next' stories

Using favourite stories, ask your child to guess how a character might react at key parts in the story. For example, when the big bad wolf appears, does Little Red Riding Hood laugh, sing a song or feel very frightened? Or when Cinderella can't go to the ball, does she smile, do a silly dance, or does she cry? This helps your child as they begin to learn empathy and also helps them to understand how we use stories to learn about feelings.

Give your child a part in the bedtime story

Ask your child to choose an animal character from the bedtime story and explain to them they have to make the noise of that character whenever they're mentioned in the story. For example, they could make a wolf noise in *Little Red Riding Hood*, or a piggie squeak in *The Three Little Pigs*. This is a chance to give your child their first ever taste of drama.

Make a first words scrapbook

During this year your child may start to use some words with meaning. A good way to praise them and celebrate their progress, as well as making a memento, is to compile a first words scrapbook. When your child first says the word 'cat' for example, you can cut out a picture of a cat, or stick in a photograph of your own pet cat and write the word in big letters alongside the date. Encourage your child to help you, and repeat it for each new word they say. You can read through the book from time to time with your child to reinforce their learning until their rate of word learning accelerates to the point where you can no longer keep up.

Insight

Some children will begin to say recognizable words in their first year. On average, an 18-month-old child can say about 50 words, but it's important to remember that your child can recognize and understand far more words than they can say.

THINGS TO DO WITH ARTS AND CRAFTS

Set up an art gallery

Find an area in your house where you can display your child's creations, be they play dough 'monsters', paintings or particularly good building block constructions. Select creations which demonstrate novelty and imagination, or ones which your child is particularly proud of. This gives your praise more currency and makes the act of displaying something special for your child.

Jackie, mum to Carla and Jo, four

'I set up a little gallery on a shelf along the stairs. When one of the twins did a new painting or made a new thing that we all really liked, we'd make a small ceremony of putting that one up, and taking the oldest thing down.'

Make potato prints

Children at this age are beginning to love patterns. The fact you can use one repeated shape to make lots of interesting new ones fascinates them. Artistically, however, children of this age struggle to repeatedly draw similar shapes. Potatoes (or other vegetables such as carrots or turnips) sliced in half with shapes cut out, make excellent biodegradable prints and they enable your child to experiment with patterns.

Make a magazine collage

Gather up some old magazines and cut out as many interesting pictures as you can. Then get some paper and a glue stick for your child and spread out the pictures so they can choose images to make a collage. The creative value in this activity comes through the process of choosing the images, so encourage your child to talk about what they found interesting about the pictures they have chosen.

Insight

When you're making things with your child, make your own picture or object too. Your child will enjoy the activity more and it will be more fun for you too.

Make glitter stones

When you're out for a walk, gather some large, fairly flat and smooth stones. Clean them up, then set out four or five bright colours of paint, some glitter and a paintbrush. The idea is that your child paints the stones, then decorates them with glitter.

Liz, mum to Tegan, four

'I put the stones I made with my daughter Tegan around the base of some plant pots. They look lovely, and because they've stayed there, everyone comments on them. She understands she's made something really beautiful.'

Make sugar pictures

Put some caster sugar into four or five plastic cups. Then add one or two drops of natural food colouring to each pot to make different shades (pale colours look very pretty). Then using glue stick and a paintbrush to dip into the sugar, help your child to paint a sugar picture.

THINGS TO MAKE FOR YOUR CHILD

Make a safe button box

Children have always loved button boxes, but at this age the problem is that it is easy for them to choke on smaller items. Use a tin or box and fill it with larger buttons, and trinkets, such as old pendants and bottle lids, which are too big for them to swallow, so they have a safe button box to rummage in and make patterns with.

Make a favourite things box

Decorate an old shoebox and give it to your child as a special treasure chest. Write their name on it, so they're fully aware it belongs to them. Then, go with them around the house to help them pick out one or two treasures, such as favourite toys, shells, bottle lids and ribbons. Then encourage them to collect new (appropriate) treasures for the box. The treasure box encourages your child to start building a sense of self through thinking and identifying things they particularly like. It is also a way of giving them their own, personal, portable space where they can express and enjoy themselves.

THINGS TO DO EVERY DAY

Create counting rituals
At some point this year your child will probably begin to use numbers. A good way to get them used to counting and to make it fun is to introduce some counting rituals into your daily routine. For example, if you have steps outside your house, you count them when you go out and come in, or whenever you build a tower with toy blocks, count how many are used.

Tidy up games
Train your child to be tidy and have fun at the same time by thinking up some games that involve tidying up. For example, when tidying building blocks, ask who can find the most blue blocks to put into the tub, then ask who can find the most green ones, etc. Another game is to get a big laundry basket or bag and ask everyone to pick up as many toys as they can and see who can put the most into the basket in 3 minutes.

Have a weather wheel
Help your child to observe the world around them and to do a little problem solving with this activity. Make a weather chart with symbols for different weather: hot, cold, sunny, windy, rainy, cloudy and snowy. Every morning, ask your child to decide which symbol best illustrates the weather outside. Then, as you're getting ready to go out, get them to help you decide what sort of things you might need to prepare for the day's weather – a warm coat, an umbrella, a woolly hat and gloves or a sun hat.

THINGS TO DO WITH TOYS

Play the sharing game
Children of this age rarely play together, but this is a game they can play independently, yet involving each other.

Each child needs to contribute three or four of his or her own toys to a basket. You then explain that every time you give the signal, each child has to pick one toy for the other child to play with for a little while. This needs to be carefully policed, and expect tears and tantrums the first few times. However, it helps children to understand that their generosity and willingness to share, should, and eventually will, be repaid. In terms of creativity, it teaches your child self-discipline and empathy, both vital ingredients in the creative process.

THINGS TO DO WITH MUSIC

Musical balls

As they develop the necessary coordination skills, toddlers love playing ball games. This game is a good way to encourage toddlers who are very physical and active to enjoy music. Choose three favourite tunes and explain to your toddler that when you play song number one, you will roll the ball to each other, when song two plays you will kick the ball to each other and when song three plays, you will throw the ball to each other.

Top tip
Play the songs for a longer time at first, then gradually change the tunes more quickly to make the game more exciting.

The magic wand dance

Another musical game is the magic wand dance. Play some music and pretend that you are a witch or wizard, and every time the music stops you will wave your magic wand and turn your child into an animal. They then have to dance or move around to the music pretending to be the animal you have turned them into.

The copy clap game

With their growing sense of rhythm and love of copying, toddlers often love this game. Start by clapping a simple rhythm, for example, three simple claps and ask them to copy you. Then try a new, slightly harder rhythm, for example one clap followed by two faster claps. Gradually increase the complexity of the rhythm.

Sing 'fill in the gap' songs

Sing favourite songs with your child and ask them to fill in the next word when you stop singing. For example, 'Twinkle twinkle, little ….'. By encouraging your child to focus on the game, they become less self-conscious about the fact they are singing.

THINGS TO DO WITH FOOD

Have a teddy bears' picnic

Encourage your child to explore new tastes and foods with an old-fashioned teddy bears' picnic. Select foods your child has not tried before, make sure you don't just put out 'good' foods, but also foods you feel fairly neutral about. Toddlers begin to understand very quickly that there are certain foods you would much prefer they ate, and that other foods are forbidden 'treats'. Often it's better if you're relaxed and not judgmental around food. Put out some roasted peppers, some popcorn, or unusual leftovers you happen to have in the fridge, and take turns with them and the teddies to try the foods and ask what each of them taste like.

Top tip

Be descriptive about the taste and texture of the food and encourage your child to be descriptive too. As well as developing language, this encourages your child to think about the different qualities of the food they are eating.

Insight

You can encourage your child to be more open to a variety of foods by giving them mashed rather than puréed food by about seven and a half months, letting them explore the textures of food and get a little messy, and giving them tasters of individual flavours.

THINGS TO DO WHICH ARE SPORTY

Have a walking backwards race

Physically, this is excellent for helping your child to use different muscle groups and gain a sense of balance. It's also a lot of fun.

Place lots of cushions around the room and have some walking backwards races. If that goes well, you might want to try some other games too, for example, counting the number of times they can jump up and down in a hoop, or a pick up the teddy race, where you have to pick up three teddies before the finishing line. All of these activities help to develop balance and coordination skills which will enable your child to be more expressive with their body.

THINGS TO DO OUTSIDE

Have a body painting session
It's often frustrating for parent and child to paint at this age. Inevitably, a lot of mess is created and it can be hard to stop yourself from constantly telling your child to be careful. On a fine day, take a big roll of paper outside, put out pots of non-toxic child's finger paint and dress yourself and your child in clothes that you don't mind getting messy. Then tell your child they can use their hands, feet, arms and legs to make a giant painting. This game is especially liberating for your child if you join in.

Have a nature treasure hunt
Find four or five 'natural treasures', for example a shell, a flower, a pine cone or a big leaf, and put shiny stickers on each thing to mark them out as treasures. Then hide them in spots around the garden where your toddler will be able to find them easily. Draw each object on a page and give your child a treasure bag to store their 'loot' in.

10 THINGS TO REMEMBER

1   *Children develop at hugely varying rates this year.*

2   *Be very descriptive in the way you talk to your child. They will develop a wider vocabulary if you use more words.*

3   *Give lots of praise to reinforce positive behaviour.*

4   *As far as reasonable, let your child choose and lead the way they play as they will learn more.*

5   *Give your child opportunities to explore new things using all five senses.*

6   *Don't feel you have to plan every moment of your child's day. Let them have some downtime.*

7   *Repetition, repetition, repetition. Babies of this age learn a lot by repeating things.*

8   *Try not to stereotype your child's toys and games according to their gender. Adult hang ups about what girls and boys should do mean nothing to babies. Let them choose if they want to wear a cowboy hat or a glittery scarf.*

9   *Involve your child in your day. Encourage them to 'help' tidy up or play at making phone calls together.*

10 *Play yourself when you're playing with them. They'll sense if you're bored and you'll both have more fun if you get involved as well.*

7

....

Two to three years

In this chapter you will learn:
- *how encouraging creativity can help your child to develop at this age*
- *the golden rules for encouraging creativity at this age*
- *activities and games which will enhance their natural curiosity and imagination.*

You will learn a lot more about your child's personality traits this year. Whether your child is a natural explorer whose dearest wish is to find new ways into forbidden territory or a child who endlessly experiments with everything from puddles to toothpaste, whether they are a happy little soul or a more serious and shy person, will all be revealed as your child takes on new challenges and tasks.

It's important to remember that even simple, everyday things in life are hugely experimental and creative for your child at this stage. Getting themselves dressed, trying different foods and visiting the supermarket are all relatively challenging and novel adventures, and it helps to try to empathize and avoid pushing your child into trying new things before they are ready. It helps a good deal to explain what you are about to do calmly and clearly in advance and give them a chance to ask questions before plunging them into a completely new situation.

In addition, be aware of how much your child takes cues from your behaviour and reaction to situations. If, for example, you seem overly anxious or worried because you are running late as you drive to nursery for the first time, your child will feel that if you are worried then perhaps there is something for them to feel anxious about too. This relates directly to your child's creative behaviour because they will feel much happier about entering new situations and trying new things out if you are relaxed and calm in the same scenario.

Finally, paying attention to your child and encouraging them to share their feelings will help them feel more confident and secure in unfamiliar situations.

Golden rules

ENCOURAGE SUCCESS

Try to set up situations where your child will be challenged but where ultimately they will probably be successful. For example, as they learn to dress themselves, break it down into small tasks, asking them to try putting on a jumper first, and praise that success. Or, if they're playing with a jigsaw, ask if they can lay the pieces picture side up first before you expect them to start putting it together. Of course in the long term, your child will need to learn the rewards of perseverance and effort and that failures help us to learn – but not yet. If your child begins to associate trying new things with a high success rate they'll feel more confident and they'll be more likely to develop the sense of adventure and experimentation that are key traits in creative people.

Insight
Remember that there is often more than one 'right way' to do things, and your child may teach you a whole new way to do an everyday task. My three-year-old son puts jigsaws together in a very different way to me, but I've discovered he does it faster!

LISTEN TO THEIR STORIES

On average, a child of two has a vocabulary of around 200 words, although of course this varies widely. But, generally speaking, they can finally begin to articulate to you a lot about their world. Simply asking interested questions will improve their confidence significantly. It is at this stage, too, that your child will begin to express fears and anxieties about the world as they start to understand that sometimes bad things can happen – they can fall and bump their head, dogs bark at them, they can feel cold and hungry. These fears and anxieties can come out in all kinds of ways, sometimes in pictures, sometimes as imaginary monsters or bogeymen. It is tempting to be a little fascinated by your child's imaginative creations, but listen for the messages underneath.

Never ridicule or dismiss fears or anxieties; instead encourage your child to confide in you. By reassuring them that you are listening and that you are on hand to help, you will make your child feel more secure. This in itself will mean your child naturally becomes more creative, imaginative and simply happier.

Insight
Children around the age of two to three often begin to develop a fear of the dark as they develop the ability to imagine, but can't yet tell the difference between fantasy and reality. You can help by using low-level night lights and showing them there are no monsters under the bed.

OVERLOOK FAILURES

At this age, your child is forming beliefs about what kind of person he or she is, based on what people tell them and how well they can complete tasks or accomplish certain skills. As a result, this stage is not the time to be dismissive or severe if your child cannot accomplish something. Of course, you want to encourage them to learn, but focus on praising effort and the fact they have tried something new. Try to be relaxed if things go wrong and you'll avoid instilling a fear of failure which could prevent them from taking on new challenges in the future. If they can't manage to draw a circle or learn to put their socks on, highlight the fact they've tried and reassure them that you know they'll eventually succeed if they keep practising.

IGNORE TANTRUMS

It's perhaps not surprising that children begin to tantrum in earnest during the 'terrible twos', screaming and crying when they can't get what they want. In their world, they have precious little control over anything, including when they have to go to sleep, what they eat, where they go and who they spend time with. Of course, that's no reason to tolerate tantrums. If your child is going to enjoy a creative, imaginative childhood, then he or she will need to develop emotional maturity. They also need to develop resourcefulness, which will not happen if they get what they want, whenever they want it. By making it clear that sometimes you do have to find other ways to resolve wants and needs, you encourage your child to use their imagination and problem-solving abilities, so they can think up new solutions or compromises.

The golden rule with tantrums is to ensure that your child is safe, and then to continue business as if the tantrum simply is not happening. It is very difficult to do this when your child is screaming loudly on the supermarket floor or won't get into their car seat when you only have 10 minutes to get to an urgent appointment. In these situations, you may have to move your child to a place where it is more appropriate for you to wait out the tantrum. But it is important for you to keep as calm as you possibly can.

If the tantrum simply doesn't end, another tactic that psychologists recommend is to teach your child how they themselves can make the tantrum 'go away' by talking to them when they are calm and teaching them to breathe deeply and count to ten slowly when they feel that a tantrum might be coming. Don't spend too much time trying to persuade them to do this during a tantrum though, as this is a substitute for attention, remind them once, then make it their job to calm themselves down.

MAKE LITTLE THINGS FUN

When you're caring for a young toddler and trying to juggle work and household chores at the same time, life is often too busy to be a 'perfect parent'. Spending hours doing creative projects with your child every day is simply unrealistic for many modern parents. However, you don't have to spend hours making your own play dough or baking specially shaped cookies to help your child become imaginative and novel in their thinking.

Your two-year-old's attention span is short anyway and with some imagination and a sense of fun, you can make even the most boring, everyday routines an adventure. Pretend the supermarket is a jungle or an underwater world, or that when they are getting into their car seat, they're actually getting into a rocket and driving through the stars on the way to Grandma's house. Even making toast can be fun if you play a game where the person who shouts 'pop!' closest to the toaster popping up is the winner.

Games, toys and activities to play with your toddler

Here are a few other ways to spend creative time with your toddler. Bear in mind that if your child isn't very interested in the activity you have set up, it is best not to force the issue, but rather to set out several different toys or materials so they can lead the play. Early Years Foundation Stage guidelines for UK child carers state that children learn far more quickly when engaging in play they have chosen themselves.

Remember: Children develop at very different paces at this age. For this reason, it's a good idea to look in the chapters before and after this one and to choose the activities and games which are most appropriate for your child.

THINGS TO DO IN THE LIVING ROOM

Tupperware city
Children of this age love ride-on toys, and if you don't have one, your local toy library might have one. Take out any plastic boxes or bowls you have and build a little city for your child to drive around. One box might be a post office, another your house; build up a stack of boxes to make an office block or put some toys in one which represents a school. If you have a tea set you could set that out next to the box which is supposed to be the café. This game encourages make-believe play and helps to develop your child's memory as they are thinking about places that you regularly visit.

The island hopping game
Set some cushions around the living room, hopping distance apart, and at the end of the trail put a big beanbag or blanket which represents a desert island. Put some treasure here, a little toy or some of your safer jewellery.

Then your child has to hop from cushion to cushion to get past the pirate or shark (you) to the treasure island. If you catch them and make them have a cuddle, they have to start again, until they manage to get to the treasure.

The memory box
A good way to help children's cognitive skills at this age is to do things which help to develop their memory. This naturally helps creativity too because people who are observant and good at remembering details gather more resources to use when they are developing new ideas or solutions.

You'll need four or five safe and interesting objects (such as a little toy, shell or necklace) and a solid box with a lid or a cotton bag. Lay out the objects on a table or mat and ask your child to look at each item and to try to remember them all. Then put the objects into the box and see how many they can remember.

THINGS TO DO OUTSIDE

Have a slide competition
Children of this age love slides and baby swings. Encourage them to use their imagination by showing you just how many different things they can do coming (safely!) down the slide. Can they lie on their tummies, on their backs, pull a funny face, make a funny noise, wiggle their fingers in the air? Take turns trying it yourself if the slide is big enough.

Plant a tree together
You'll need a small potted tree (these are available from garden centres or online from websites such as www.treesdirect.co.uk), compost, a watering can, card, string and sticky tape.

Ask your child to help you dig a hole big enough for the roots of your tree. Ensure the earth at the bottom is loose and damp. Plant your tree and with your child, surround the roots with compost, pat the earth down, and ask your child to give the tree some water.

THINGS TO DO EVERY DAY

Let them choose their clothes

This is not an activity which is suitable if you need to leave the house quickly. However, on days when you do not have to rush, giving your child choice increases their self-esteem as well as encourages them to think creatively about what they wear.

Lay out three different pairs of trousers (or skirts), three tops and three pairs of socks and ask them to choose one item from each pile to wear today. When they're ready, let them start trying to dress themselves.

Diane, mum to Ruby, five

'When Ruby was about this age, I organized her clothes into little baskets under her bed – one basket of tops, one of skirts and trousers and one of socks and tights. She used to love going to each basket and picking out her "outfit". She looked ridiculous fairly often, but it was a lot of fun and really made her feel independent.'

CASE STUDY

Do some 2-minute meditation

When your child is feeling calm or slightly sleepy, lie down next to each other and ask them to close their eyes while you imagine walking together somewhere peaceful and beautiful. Cuddle them or hold their hand so they feel safe and ask them what sort of place they might like to imagine. Then describe different aspects of the place exploring all the senses. For example, if your child wanted to imagine the seaside, talk about the soft sand under their feet and the sound of waves lapping gently on the shore. Meditation helps your child to learn to calm themselves and to visualize relaxing, happy places when they need comfort.

In terms of creativity, meditation helps you to achieve a calm level of alpha brain waves which are believed to foster the beginnings of the creative process.

Insight

According to psychologist David Fontana, author of *Teaching Meditation to Children*, meditation can help your child in improving concentration, establishing emotional balance and enhancing imagination and creativity.

THINGS TO DO WHEN YOU'RE OUT AND ABOUT

Have a colour day
Choose a day to have a special colour day. Ask your toddler to choose their favourite colour and theme your day around it. For example, if it's a yellow day, eat yellow food, like bananas and custard, wear something yellow, buy some yellow flowers, or pick up yellow leaves you see. Cut out pictures from a magazine with yellow in them to make a yellow collage and play a game where you think of as many yellow things as you can.

Play the supermarket colour sweep
Whenever you put something brightly coloured into your trolley, ask your child to shout out the colour (you might need to add bananas to your list to ensure you include yellow, or a red onion for purple). Your child will probably get bored for periods of time, follow their lead and don't force the issue, but do try reviving the game if a tantrum threatens.

Planes and boats and trains

Every so often plan a little adventure on a mode of transport your child has never been on before. It could be the top deck of a double-decker bus, a ferry ride or a ride on a train. Make an adventure of it, and talk about what you're going to do; take a camera and a picnic and keep mementos such as tickets to put into a 'travel journal' when you get home.

THINGS TO DO WITH ARTS AND CRAFTS

Shape painting

Cut differently coloured card into triangles, circles, squares and rectangles and ask your child to make a picture out of them. Sit nearby and make a few pictures of your own so they can get ideas from you if they wish.

Have a 'favourite things' picture gallery

Your child will begin to show a clear preference for certain toys or characters from books or TV programmes now. They may also have favourite friends and pets. Put up some pictures of some of their favourite things along a picture rail or on one wall in their bedroom and encourage them to think of more things to add to it every so often. It's a way of helping them to gain a sense of identity as well as thinking about how to express that in a visual way.

Make pasta wigs

You will need:

- ▶ *dried penne pasta*
- ▶ *paint and paintbrushes*
- ▶ *card*
- ▶ *child-friendly scissors*
- ▶ *string*
- ▶ *glue or masking tape.*

With your child, paint lots of dried pasta shapes and leave them to dry. Then, cut out a saucer-sized circle of card, fold it in half twice then cut a little hole, about the size of a five pence piece, in the middle.

Next, cut out a V shape from the edges towards the middle, but not quite reaching the hole. Make this V about the width of your child's forehead.

Cut the string into roughly 25-centimetre (10 inch) sections, (or however long you want your 'hair' to be plus 5 centimetres (2 inches), then thread each section with the pasta shapes, leaving 5 centimetres (2 inches) free at the top.

Then take each piece of string and thread the spare 5 centimetres through the hole in the centre of your card and stick down to the underside with sticky tape. Leave even spaces between each piece of string and leave a gap at the V shape you have cut out. The end result should be a colourful pasta wig.

Make balloon monsters
Blow up six or seven coloured balloons and, with your child, draw lots of different faces on them with felt-tip pens.

Make a mobile
You will need:

> ▶ *2 plastic coat hangers*
> ▶ *some string and sticky tape*
> ▶ *objects of your choice, such as feathers, bells, bottle lids*
> ▶ *or pieces of coloured card cut into interesting shapes.*

First, stick the two coat hangers together firmly at right angles to each other with sticky tape. Then, cut out eight or ten different lengths of string and tie thick knots at the end. Then thread or stick your objects onto each piece of string, ensuring there is something heavy at the bottom of the string, and working up. Stick or tie the string to the coat hangers and display.

Make a life-size monster

Unravel about 1.5 metres from a roll of paper and ask your toddler to lie down on it. Then draw around your toddler. When you have finished the outline, help your child to draw monster horns and fangs, or whatever other elements they would like to have on their 'monster', then cut him out to stick up on the wall.

THINGS TO DO WITH MUSIC

The witch and the fairy

This game is a variation of musical statues which encourages children to express themselves through dance and also stimulates make-believe play.

Tell your child that you are pretending to be a witch or wizard and your child is a fairy or an elf dancing in the garden. As long as the magical music is playing, the witch can't hear or see the fairies, but when it stops, she can, so fairies have to stand perfectly still until the music comes on again. If a child moves and the witch sees them she'll turn them into a toad.

Have a dance session

At this age, children are beginning to enjoy a real sense of rhythm and move in time to the music. Every so often, put on some of their favourite songs and just dance together. Let them see you're enjoying yourself, and they'll be less self-conscious.

Mirror dancing

Put on some lively music and play this game with both of you facing the mirror. You make a movement, then they have to copy you and dance in the same way. They'll love watching themselves and will also have to work out how to move their body in the right direction to copy you.

Make your own 'musical'

Using one of your child's favourite stories, find three or four different instruments (or instruments fashioned from things around the house) to play when different characters come along in the story. For example, a big deep drum can be Mr Wolf, a little shaky tambourine can be a scared little piggy or a sleigh bell could be a fairy.

This encourages your child to think about the different qualities of characters and the ways sounds can represent them.

Make a music blanket
You will need another grown-up or an older sibling to help with this. Find a blanket or sheet and the two adults hold it up high and gradually move it down low over your toddler and then up high again, singing lower notes as the blanket moves down and higher notes as the blanket is lifted. This is a fun game for your child and a good way to teach them about pitch.

Do a food dance
This is a good way to get your child to think in an 'off the wall' abstract kind of way. Put on some music and encourage your child to dance; then stop the music and shout out the name of some food. For the next session of music your child has to dance like a banana, or spaghetti, or whichever food you have called out.

THINGS TO DO WITH BOOKS

Start a scrapbook
Another way to strengthen memory and to encourage creative thinking is to start a scrapbook for your child. Start them off by sticking in some pictures of an outing, for example, a visit to the zoo, then encourage your child to gather a few objects for the book – tickets and other mementos of the day. If you've been to the woods, you might want to stick in leaves or flowers, or shells to record a visit to the seaside. Every so often, read through the scrapbook with your child, and show it to other people, so your child gets another helping of praise and attention for their creative endeavour.

Draw a story

At some point this year, your child may start to try drawing familiar objects and people. Read them a favourite story, then ask them to draw a picture of it for you. The things your child draws probably won't look anything like what they say each thing is, but ask them questions about the colours they've used and what the different things are. This activity helps them to use their imagination to visualize the characters and scenes in stories. It will give you a fascinating insight into their mind.

Make a visitors' book

This book encourages your child to remember things and also gives them a creative way to express themselves.

Buy a scrapbook or journal and use it to record visits to your home. For each visit write down the name of the visitor, the date, and include a picture of your visitor if possible. Then leave some blank space for your child to stick things in, draw pictures or to say words that you can write into the book for them so they can remember the visit and talk about it later.

THINGS TO DO WITH FOOD

Have a Martian dinner

Make a dinner with a difference; use natural food colourings to make blue mashed potatoes or pink toast (paint on diluted food colouring with a pastry brush). As well as being fun and imaginative, it will encourage your child to think about the taste and textures of the food.

Grow a cress monster
You will need:

▶ *a white pot or a pot that has white paper around it*
▶ *a marker pen*
▶ *cotton wool or kitchen roll*
▶ *cress seeds.*

Draw your monster face on the outside of the pot. Fill the pot with some kitchen roll or cotton wool until it almost reaches the top. Then add water until it feels slightly damp. Sprinkle your cress or mustard seeds on top then place the pot in a warm place. In a few days you'll have a hairy green cress monster. Cut the cress and enjoy a cress sandwich to introduce your child to the benefits of home-grown food.

Mashed potato sculptures
Most families tend to have a rule that you 'shouldn't play with food', but during this activity the idea is that you're not going to eat the food. It's just a different medium to play with that's not harmful if it goes into your child's mouth. It might be more convenient to use powdered mash for this game.

Put a big plastic bowl of mashed potato onto a covered table and make sculptures using hands, plastic spoons, knives, forks and any other suitable items. This activity is also a good way for your child to see how in certain circumstances, where everyone is safe and no harm or inconvenience is being caused, it can be appropriate to break the rules.

Make fruit and vegetable pictures
Cut out slices of different kinds of fruit and vegetables and show your child how to make different pictures out of it. For example, a peach slice and a carrot stick can make a little boat, with a slice of banana or lemon as the sun. You can snack on your art materials as you go along.

10 THINGS TO REMEMBER

1 *Explain what you're going to do when you're starting a new activity so your child feels safer and more prepared.*

2 *Your child will pick up on your feelings about something you're going to do, whether that is anxiety, boredom or calm and positivity.*

3 *Set your child up for success. Choose games and tasks that they will do well at to encourage good self-esteem.*

4 *Listen to your child, and ask them questions about what they tell you. You'll earn back trust and respect by giving it, and in turn they'll feel more comfortable sharing their thoughts and imagination with you.*

5 *Don't be too hard on them when they fail at things. Your child is learning to do so many things we take for granted.*

6 *Tantrums are a means of getting you to change your behaviour so your child gets their own way in terms of treats, attention or some other reward. Make sure your child is safe, try to stay calm and withdraw attention from them until they calm down.*

7 *Parents of young toddlers are so busy, so put fun and magic into little moments of the day such as car journeys, saying 'hello' after time apart and first thing in the morning.*

8 *Talk to your child about things they've seen and done during their day, as this helps to improve their memory.*

9 *Give your toddler choices wherever you can. So much of their world is controlled, so let them choose their clothes, or how to come down the slide (safely) whenever you can.*

10 *Do things that you enjoy with your child, for example, meditation, dancing or gardening.*

8

Three to four years

In this chapter you will learn:
- *how encouraging creativity can help your child to develop at this age*
- *the golden rules for encouraging creativity at this age*
- *activities and games which will enhance their natural curiosity and imagination.*

As your child passes the landmark age of three, their imagination will really take flight. These are the really magical years when make believe and fantasy play a huge part in your child's life. As well as the natural curiosity and wonderful creativity of children at this stage, they also learn to stop putting things in their mouths and develop more cognitive skills and physical abilities. The result is that a whole new world opens up for you in terms of the fun and imaginative things you can do together.

For many parents, it's also the last year before your child starts school, so you still have a little more time and freedom to plan activities and games.

Your child will be enthusiastic to join in. At this age, children love climbing and crawling and swinging and sliding as they test out their quickly developing motor skills. They are fascinated by the world around them, asking questions about everything, many of which will be so original that they will make you see the world in a new way too.

If they haven't already, your child may also begin to express their sense of humour, laughing at silly jokes and funny sounds and faces. Three-year-olds are a real joy to spend time with because this is also the age at which long-term memories begin to form; it's a time when you can begin to encourage long-lasting habits and mindsets, and instil a lifelong love of learning, exploration and experimentation.

At this age, children are still in the formative phase of development, they are less likely to wish to follow the herd and copy everything their peers do, as they will when they progress to the normative phase of childhood. This is a good age to teach your child that individuality is something to celebrate.

Golden rules

YOU CAN'T FORCE CREATIVITY

Most three-year-olds are instinctively curious and imaginative. However, as renowned psychologist Vygotsky once famously quoted, 'Creativity cannot be forced'. If your child doesn't want to play along with make believe or paint their own picture, don't push them to do it.

What you can do to nurture and encourage their creative instincts is to be very non-judgemental, yet interested about things they do create, and to give them plenty of opportunities, ideas and access to resources to stimulate creativity. Also, give your child opportunities to observe you being creative.

MAKE SURE YOU ASK THE QUESTIONS

A common theme in children this age is that they are forever asking 'Why?'. The why circle can end up with you trying to explain exactly why the sun is yellow without going into astrophysics. An easy and effective way to escape the why game without stifling their curiosity is to simply turn the questions around. For example, if your child asks, 'What colour is the sea?' simply reply, 'What colour do you think the sea is?' Or if they ask 'Why?' ask them, 'Why do you think that happens?' It breaks the annoying why cycle and also encourages your child to think about things for themselves.

> ## Insight
>
> When you ask your child to come up with their own answers to their questions, you'll often find they have a theory, often a very off-the-wall and interesting one, which gives you a whole new insight into their budding personality and what they actually meant by the question.

COPYING IS OK

A major myth about creativity is that it's wrong to copy. Actually, copying, when it's a re-interpretation of another child's picture, or a re-telling of a story in their own words, is quite a creative process. When your child does this, they are taking something into their world and reforming ideas and thoughts, and then expressing their reinvention. However, if a child is copying because they don't know what else to do, or are afraid to do something for themselves, you'll need to reassure them that there is no 'right way' to do something and to encourage them to produce something a little more original.

PLAY ALONG WITH MAKE BELIEVE

It is easy for adults to be very dismissive and separate from the world of childhood fantasy and imagination. Adults often behave this way unwittingly, through the use of sarcastic responses along the lines of: 'I suppose the fairies ate that biscuit then did they?' At other times, parents resist their children's urges to pretend to ride a horse around the living room because they feel silly. Children are very intuitive, and they pick up on the embarrassment and scepticism which adults sometimes show when it comes to make believe. Yet by trying to be a part of that world, you will actively encourage your child to explore their fantasy world and stretch their imagination. Show them exactly how to pretend to be an aeroplane during take off and landing and ask them about the imaginary friends who often appear by this age.

Insight

During this year your child will begin to be able to tell the difference between what's real and what's make believe, but even so, they'll enjoy suspending their disbelief for many years to come.

DON'T HELP UNLESS THEY ASK

Children at this age often insist they must do things 'all by myself!' This natural assertion of independence is very beneficial, as it not only enables them to develop more quickly, but also gives them a huge sense of achievement and self-confidence when they do accomplish something unaided. Try to step back a bit. Don't tell your child what colours things should be in their painting, and resist the urge to comment when they put a puzzle piece in upside down. Now is the time to let them come up with their own inventions and solutions to problems.

Insight

A good way to discourage yourself from being too quick to help is to try doing a puzzle or making a simple picture yourself and asking them to help you. Inevitably they'll want to do it all their own way, and you'll discover first hand how annoying this can be if it is 'your' picture.

MAKE SURE THEY HAVE ENOUGH DOWNTIME

Children of this age have not yet begun their full-time education, and yet many three-year-olds have incredibly hectic schedules. Aside from daycare or nursery, there are ballet lessons, baby gymnastic sessions, music classes and swimming courses to name but a few regular activities available for preschool children. Many children have activities planned every day. One study by the Survey Research Centre at the University of Michigan documented that between 1981 and 1997, children aged three to 12 lost on average 12 hours per week of free time.

Yet, many experts believe that simple, everyday activities, such as spending time talking to your child or enjoying longer family mealtimes, can be more beneficial to your child than taking them to organized activities. For example, the University of Michigan study of how children spend their time found that more mealtimes at home was the strongest predictor of better achievement scores and fewer behavioural problems. Another study by the American Academy of Paediatrics indicated that over-scheduling can lead to increased stress and anxiety.

Top tip

Ask your child to help you lay the table and put their own cutlery, plates and cups out. It provides a transition for them from the previous activity, and makes them feel more involved in the daily ritual.

Games, toys and activities to play with your curious and creative toddler

Here are some games and activities which will help to foster your child's creativity at this age. If your child isn't very interested in the activity you have set up, it is best not to force the issue, but rather to set out several different toys or materials so they can lead the play.

Remember: Children develop at different paces. For this reason it's a good idea to look in the chapters before and after this one and to choose the activities and games which are most appropriate for your child.

THINGS TO DO WITH COMPUTERS

Top tip

Many researchers agree that computers do not match the learning style of children under the age of three. Until this age, children learn best from physical interaction with real things and by exploring using all five senses.

However, studies, such as that by Dr Susan Haugland of the Metropolitan State College of Denver in 1992, reveal that children aged three and four who use computers in an appropriate way can develop more quickly than those who don't. As a result of these studies, the American Academy of Paediatrics concludes that computers help children of this age to build memory skills and to increase creativity. Guidelines state that children should have an adult on hand to help when required and that they should spend no more than one hour a day at the computer. Age-appropriate software should be used.

Insight

When choosing games for children of this age, avoid ones which involve using the mouse as your child won't have the fine motor skills needed for that yet, so stick to ones which involve hitting any key or the space bar.

Play PC peek-a-boo

Many adults believe computer games stifle the imagination, and for older children this can be true. But computers are also a source of very well-designed games and activities which have been created specifically to develop children's cognitive and creative abilities, and there are many resources available for very young preschool children. As well as enjoying the games, your child will also be gaining familiarity with computers – a skill vital in the modern world. Your child will also be interacting with you as they play, letting you know how they are progressing.

www.kneebouncers.com is a good website for children of this age.
Toddlers can hit any key and cause music and drums to sound.
There is also a game where hitting the keyboard makes bubbles rise
up onto the screen.

www.fisher-price.com also has a well-designed children's zone
where, among other games, your child can hit the keyboard and
play online peek-a-boo.

www.bbc.co.uk/cbeebies have similar games where your toddler
can play peek-a-boo and listen to nursery rhymes and songs.

Computer colouring
As children this age are still mastering the motor skills to colour in
well, a good way to encourage them to enjoy technology and do
some excellent colouring in is to use some of the online colouring
games for toddlers. Websites such as www.webtots.co.uk and
www.fisher-price.com have a tap and colour game designed to suit
a range of developmental stages. For example, there are games
suitable for children who can hit the space bar. Other games are
suitable for those who are learning to use the mouse.

Play with a mouse
Your toddler will have the fine motor skills now to move a computer
mouse around and watch how it affects things on screen. As yet,
however, it may be difficult for them to hold the mouse still and
click on specific objects. Games such as the Underwater World on
www.webtots.co.uk and Reader Rabbit toddler games (available
from Amazon at www.amazon.co.uk) feature 'clickless' games which
are designed so that your child will cause responses when they
move the mouse pointer over objects on the screen.

Online artists
When your child's fine motor skills have developed to the
point where they can use a mouse and click on the right spot
on the computer screen, there are a wide range of artistic
games and activities available. Websites such as Cbeebies
www.bbc.co.uk/cbeebies and www.coloring.com have lots of free

and carefully designed colouring pages where your child can click on a colour, and then the area they want to paint. One of the key benefits of online colouring this way is that your child can easily change the colours they have chosen several times to experiment with different effects.

THINGS TO MAKE FOR YOUR CHILD

Face paints
You can of course get your child's face painted with beautiful designs representing lions and butterflies at many events, but it's much more fun to have a homespun face-painting session, where you both paint each others faces. Avoid getting paint near the eyes of course, and don't carry out this activity if your child has cuts or sensitive skin!

You will need:

▶ *1 tsp of cornstarch*
▶ *1/2 tsp of aqueous or cold cream*
▶ *1/2 tsp of water*
▶ *natural food colourings*
▶ *an old plate*
▶ *a few dry sponges*
▶ *paintbrushes*
▶ *a big mirror.*

Mix the cornstarch and cream together then add in the water until you have the right consistency. Then using an old plate, make a palette so you can mix the different colours you want using food colourings.

Start by sponging on a light base, and gradually add darker colours with a paintbrush to build up your design.

THINGS TO ENCOURAGE MAKE-BELIEVE PLAY

Paint a mural for your child's room
Ask your child to suggest things they might like painted on their wall. It could be just a few butterflies or flowers on the

wall, or a moon and stars and space rocket flying across the ceiling, to a full wall complete with pirate ship and desert island. If you don't feel artistically able to paint your own pictures, there are lots of mural stickers and kits available. For example, wallpaper murals of everything from tropical beaches to unicorns and princesses are available to purchase at websites such as www.wallpapermurals.co.uk. Removable wall sticker sets such as the 'under the sea' set are available to purchase at www.childrens-rooms.co.uk.

Top tip
Make sure that the mural is empty of characters and a scene your child can use as a backdrop in make-believe games.

Make a cardboard box rocket
Try to save one or two big boxes after Christmas, birthdays or a new furniture delivery. Pull apart the card and bend one sheet into a large tube, and another into a cone shape for the rocket nose. Stick it together and cut out a door.

Then ask your child to help you to finish the rocket using old cereal boxes and plastic containers to make wings, windows or whatever else your child might want to add. Then you can paint the rocket together.

Build a toy town
Raid the recycling box or collect old boxes and containers and place a large piece of card down on the table. Then tell your child you're going to build a little town for them to use for their dolls or cars, or any other toys of their choice. Ask them which houses and shops they might like to have in their town and set them out along the streets of the new toy town.

THINGS TO DO IN THE LIVING ROOM

Cleaning up games
Put some newspaper or a waterproof cover on a table, and give your child a small bowl of warm, soapy water and a sponge. Then ask if they can help you to clean some pots and pans. Other ways

to enable them to join in with housework are to give your child a little duster so they can polish where you've cleaned, or to ask them to sweep up ahead as you vacuum.

Put on a shadow puppet show
Shine a strong torch at an empty section of wall, close the curtains and put on a shadow puppet show together. You can show your child how to use their fingers to make birds, rabbits, dogs or wiggly worms. Ask your child to create their own creatures too.

THINGS TO DO OUTSIDE

Create a flower or vegetable garden
Mark out a little plot of the garden, or fill a pot with compost and help your child to plant some seeds. Encourage your child to water their garden daily and help them to nurture their plot, rooting out weeds, so your child can enjoy watching their seedlings grow. If you're not that green fingered, buy some seedlings from your local garden centre and gradually add in other items, such as ornaments or rain bells as the garden grows.

> **Top tip**
> Don't be tempted to give your child the most neglected corner of your garden for their patch. If the soil isn't good and nothing grows they will soon lose interest.

The giant bubble experiment
You will need:

- *a bucket or deep tray*
- *9 cups of cold water*
- *8 tbsp of glycerine*
- *1 cup of child's shampoo (for tear-free bubbles) or cheap washing-up liquid*
- *1 old wire coat hanger.*

> **Top tip**
> If you can't get hold of glycerine, use sugar instead.

Mix the water, glycerine and washing-up liquid/shampoo together, skimming any foam off the top. Then untwist the coat hanger and bend it into a wand with a saucer sized loop at the top and show your child how you can make huge, enormous bubbles. To add to the experiment, you can use something such as a fly swatter to make lots of little bubbles.

Top tip

Try adding food colouring to make coloured bubbles. These can stain things when they pop, so this is best done outside.

Make sand sculptures

This activity can be done in a sandpit, but ideally it's best to do it at the beach, where there's plenty of sand and water to hand. Make sure you've got lots of containers and shaping tools – not just buckets and spades. Use Tupperware pots, old plant pots, anything that's unusually shaped. Spoons and the ends of paintbrushes are useful sand sculpting tools.

Dampen the sand, or dig down to the wet sand if you are at the beach. Eight parts dry sand to one part water is ideal if you are using play sand and water. Pat down a firm base and ask your child to suggest the shape you will make together. Then add sand to form the rough shape. Then, working from the top down, pat the sand until it is firm, mould it and carve out the fine detail of your sculpture. Don't forget to take pictures if you have your camera.

Make handprint and footprint pictures

This activity is best done outside on a sunny day!

You'll need a roll of paper, some plastic trays and lots of paint. Roll out the paper and make sure your child is in old clothes. Then show them how, by dipping their hands into the paint, they can use the handprints to make lots of different pictures, such as flowers, trees and suns. Encourage them to play and experiment. Then do the same with feet, walking one foot in front of the other to make a snake, or creating feet people. If your child starts finger painting, or rolling around, relax and let them create their own picture in their own way.

Paint balloons
You will need:

▶ *balloons*
▶ *string*
▶ *pins or sticky tape*
▶ *lots of newspaper*
▶ *a roll of paper*
▶ *bottles of paint*
▶ *plastic forks.*

Tie a line of string to posts or trees. Lay lots of newspaper on the floor underneath. Then pour different colours of paint into different balloons and blow them up.

Hang the balloons from the string, then roll out your painting paper underneath them. The game is to pop the balloons and make a splatter picture. Remember to wear old clothes for this one too!

Have a garden safari
Make sure you have a camera, magnifying glass, a jam jar with pierced lid and a garden wildlife book. Explain to your child that you are going to see what interesting creatures and animals you might find in your garden or local park. Talk to them about some of the creatures they might see, and reassure them if they are scared of any particular creatures that you will avoid them. Then discuss the route you will take and explain that they must be very quiet as you walk and gentle with any creatures they see.

Set off, looking for little ants, ladybirds, wild birds or spiders. Take some pictures if you can. You might want to scoop a little grasshopper or caterpillar into the jar for a brief close look before setting it free again. When you find an animal, look it up in your book and talk about it.

THINGS TO DO WHEN YOU ARE OUT AND ABOUT

Go on a mystery tour
Make an outing more fun by telling your child that you are taking them on a magical mystery tour. Make a ticket for your child entitling them to a ride on the Magical Mystery Tour a few days in advance and begin to give them some clues as to where you might be going.

Plan the day carefully, organizing meals or stops at interesting places along the way to build up the suspense.

THINGS TO DO EVERY DAY

Talk about their day
Another way to encourage storytelling and to reinforce memory is to talk about your child's day with them during the bedtime routine. Start at the beginning and ask them to remind you of all the things you did together today, and talk about what the best parts of the day were. Focussing on the happier moments is also a way to encourage pleasant dreams.

THINGS TO DO WITH ARTS AND CRAFTS

Make papier mâché planets
You will need:

- *115 g/4 oz flour*
- *1.5 pints of water*
- *newspaper*
- *paintbrush*
- *balloons*
- *paint.*

Gradually add the water to the flour and mix it together with the paintbrush. Then inflate a balloon. Tear strips of newspaper and dip them into the mixture you've made, scraping off any surplus.

Layer the sticky strips over the balloon. Continue until the balloon is covered with several layers of newspaper.

Leave it to dry overnight. The next day, pop the balloon by sticking a pin through the papier mâché, and paint your planets any colours you like.

Take photos

Buy a cheap digital camera, or one specially designed for children, such as the V-Tech Kidizoom digital camera, or the Fisherprice Kid Tough Waterproof camera. If funds are low, you can often get old digital cameras from friends and family, or from www.freecycle.com – an online community where people give away old things they don't want to sell or throw away.

Your child will have developed the motor skills to take pictures, but might find it easier to use an LCD display rather than looking through the viewfinder. Encourage them to take some pictures, and ask your child to select a few to be printed out.

Top tip

Many parents are wary of allowing their children to use digital cameras, and childproof versions can be costly. However, it is recommended you provide a digital camera rather than a disposable one for the following reasons:

▶ *The cost of developing the film is prohibitive as many shots taken by children will be out of focus and blurred. On one disposable camera with just 24 exposures, they may not get any good shots at all and that will be expensive and very discouraging.*
▶ *With digital cameras the child can probably take some relatively good pictures and the rest can be deleted. That is more rewarding for them and less expensive.*
▶ *They can also look on the LCD screen and see the photo they are taking more easily. Little children find it hard to look through a viewfinder.*

Make a magazine

You will need:

- ▶ *plain paper*
- ▶ *a hole punch*
- ▶ *string*
- ▶ *old magazines*
- ▶ *photos, stickers*
- ▶ *scissors*
- ▶ *glue.*

Bind some paper together using a hole punch and some string. Then help your child to stick a big picture of themselves on the front page and write the name they choose for the magazine. Inside, stick down any pictures your child chooses and ask them to help choose some words to go with the pictures. Leave space for other elements such as drawings or stickers.

The soldier factory

This is a game designed to help shy children get more involved and extrovert children to listen more carefully. It also teaches children about teamwork.

Explain to your child you are going to make a group of toy fairies or soldiers, but because you're making so many, you're going to do it in a little production line of two or three children. Explain to each child how to make just one part of the fairy or soldier. For example, one child learns how to stencil and/or cut out the body, one child learns how to make fairy wings from silver paper, and the third learns how to stick them all together at the end.

Observe the process, without getting too deeply involved in helping. Soon each child will want to be involved in each of the different stages of production, and as a result, the louder children will need to listen to the quieter of the group, whilst the more introverted children will be encouraged to talk and lead the conversation.

Make a butterfly mobile

You will need:

- ▶ *3 pieces of A4 plain card*
- ▶ *paint*
- ▶ *glue*
- ▶ *glitter for decoration*
- ▶ *pipe cleaners*
- ▶ *needle and thick thread*
- ▶ *3 twigs or pieces of dowling.*

Fold two of the A4 cards in half and cut down the fold. Then, with each half, fold in half again and draw one wing of a butterfly on one side, so the centre of the body is at the fold in the card. Cut around the outside of your drawing to get your butterfly shape. Repeat so you have four butterfly shapes.

On the third piece of card, draw eight butterfly bodies with little heads. Then paint them with your child. Next, paint and decorate the butterfly wings. When they're dry, stick the bodies to each side of the wings in the middle so you have your four butterflies. Make two holes in the head of each one and thread pipe cleaners through for antennae.

Tie a piece of string around the centre of your first twig. This will be used to hang the mobile. Pull some knotted thread through the balancing point of the first butterfly (somewhere along its middle) and tie it firmly to one end of the first twig or piece of dowling. Then tie the second butterfly to the other end of that twig. Get your second and third twigs and tie butterflies to both ends of those twigs. Then, loop some string around the centre of the twigs and tie them to the centre of the twigs above, to make T shapes. The final shape should resemble a family tree.

Press flowers
Go for a stroll around your garden with your child or take a trip to the local flower shop to chose some flowers. Then, make sure each flower is clean, dry and trimmed of any excess bits that will make it hard to flatten. Then fold it into some blotting paper and between the pages of an old telephone directory. Then heap lots of heavy books on the top and simply leave it for three or four weeks. You might want to mark on the calendar when the flower needs to be removed.

Alternatively, a faster modern day way to press flowers is to use the microwave. You can buy special microwave flower presses from most craft shops.

Make a junk collage
Set out lots of different boxes, containers, buttons, ribbons, bits of paper, tissue, paint and glue on the table with paintbrushes. Set down newspapers to protect from mess.

Then sit with your child and let them create whatever they wish to, making suggestions or helping only if your child asks you or seems to be getting frustrated.

THINGS TO DO WITH MUSIC

Dressing up to music game
Place a pile of clothes, lots of hats, gloves, baggy shirts and shoes, in the middle of the room and play some fast music. You and your child have to put as many clothes on as you can before the music stops. The winner is the one who has the most clothes on at the end. It's a good way to encourage children who aren't naturally inclined to be inventive, as they'll put together a really funny outfit without even stopping to think about it.

Make up a sun dance
Your child is really good at moving to the music now. Encourage expression through music and movement by suggesting they make up their own special dance. On a rainy day, tell them about the Native Americans and how they used to do special dances when they wanted it to rain. Show them how it was done, pacing or skipping around in a circle, maybe making rain movements with your fingers and chanting. Then suggest your child might like to make up a sun dance. Have a selection of music ready in case they'd like to pick a song, and then think up some sunny moves together, for example, making big circles with their hands, smiling and thinking about the kinds of movements you might make on a sunny day.

Have a recording session
Ask your child to choose a favourite song, and then to practise singing it a few times with you. Then, record your song using a voice recorder or tape recorder and play it back to them. You may want to add some backing music using children's karaoke CDs or your own musical instruments.

Make a CD together
Children can really surprise you with the different kinds of music they love at this age, before peer pressure takes effect.

Play different songs in the car or at home for a week. During this time, ask your child to choose songs they would like you to put on a CD for them. Put the finished CD in a case, print out the title tracks and put their picture and name on the cover.

THINGS TO DO WITH BOOKS

Play the letter game
This is a good activity for three-year-olds who are beginning to write their first letters. Find four or five different objects all beginning with the same letter, and ask your child to guess what letter it is. For example, a lettuce, a lamp and a picture of a ladybird. The next part of the game is for them to try to write the letter. Finally, ask them to think of as many things as they can that also start with that letter.

Put on a play
Lots of children this age might nervously appear in the playgroup Nativity play, or a preschool play, but they are far more likely to enjoy putting on a show at home for people they trust and know well. Use a favourite nursery rhyme or story, using just three or four scenes and a very short script of two or three words per scene. Then practise with them and encourage them to act out their play for a close friend or relative. You can help backstage with costumes and prompting.

Write your child their own story
When your child reaches a stage when they have an important lesson they need to learn, for example, learning to share their toys, or learning to control their temper tantrums, make up a story to help them to understand the lesson using your child as the lead character. If you don't want to make up your own story, adapt a fairytale or fable which will help to illustrate the lesson they need to learn. For example, the Aesops fable, about the dog in the manger who refuses to share his comfortable bed and ends up with no friends, will help your child to understand why it is important to share.

THINGS TO DO WITH FOOD

Cupcake characters
Make 12 fairy cakes using the following recipe:

- ▶ *12 cake cases*
- ▶ *125 g/4.5 oz butter*
- ▶ *125 g/4.5 oz caster sugar*
- ▶ *2 eggs*
- ▶ *1 tsp vanilla extract*
- ▶ *125 g/4.5 oz self-raising flour*
- ▶ *2 tbsp milk.*

Preheat the oven to 190°C, gas mark 5 and put the fairy cake cases into the baking tray. Using a fork, cream the butter and sugar together until fluffy, then whisk in the eggs and vanilla extract. Fold half the flour into the mixture, then add the milk and the rest of the flour. Stir until the mixture pours very slowly off a spoon and distribute it evenly into the cake cases. Cook for around 12 minutes or until the cakes have risen and are golden. Cool on a rack until the cakes are no longer warm to touch.

ICING
Use ready-to-roll icing, or firm icing you've made yourself by adding water to icing sugar.

Think of the animal/character you want to create and add natural food colouring to create the icing you will need. For example, use the cooled cupcakes as the body for your cupcake monster and add heads, legs and other features from your icing – balls of icing for big noses and eyes and cutting out icing fangs. Let your child decide what they want to make.

Make a pasta snake
You will need:

- ▶ *penne pasta*
- ▶ *sliced olives*

- *sliced peppers*
- *pesto or tomato pasta sauce.*

Cook the penne pasta and drain it. Then set out the warm pasta in a bowl and with your child, make the shape of a long, wiggly snake, two penne deep, with a few put together to make the shape of the head. Decorate the snake with the olives and sliced peppers and finally drizzle over the pesto or tomato sauce to 'colour in' his body.

10 THINGS TO REMEMBER

1 *Encourage lots of questions but don't think you have to know all the answers!*

2 *Children of this age laugh ten times more than adults. Join in!*

3 *Teach your child that it's OK to be different.*

4 *Remember, you can't force creativity, and you should never make it a chore.*

5 *It's OK to copy, so long as it's not because you're afraid to try something new.*

6 *Don't be cynical about your child's make-believe world.*

7 *Don't help to much. Step back and try not to interfere in their play unless they ask.*

8 *Give your child some free time.*

9 *Computers can be a useful resource for children of this age if used in the right way, for short periods of time.*

10 *Home-spun activities such as DIY face paints or murals are fun, but parents of children this age face huge demands on their time, and it's better to have shop-bought activities and a calm, happy parent!*

9

Four to five years

In this chapter you will learn:
- *how encouraging creativity can help your child to develop at this age*
- *the golden rules for encouraging creativity at this age*
- *activities and games which will enhance their natural curiosity and imagination.*

Your child is becoming increasingly independent, imaginative and curious this year. As they master fine motor skills they can draw pictures in ever increasing detail as well as dressing themselves. However, although their skills are developing quickly, they can often feel frustrated when they can't master new skills straight away. And although your child is getting better at mastering their emotions, you'll still see plenty of tantrums when a paper aeroplane won't fly or maybe see your child changing their minds about the object they are drawing because 'it doesn't look right'.

> ### Insight
> Try not to be too much of a perfectionist yourself around your children when they are this age. Show that it's OK to make mistakes while you're learning new things.

Art and creativity are something children love at this age, and many are learning that they can express sadness or anger in their paintings, models, through imaginary play or by making up their own stories or songs.

138

While children of this age demonstrate their blossoming creativity in a huge variety of ways, sometimes this can manifest itself in forms of bad behaviour. For example, many children tend to start exaggerating and boasting at this age and find new, boisterous ways to exploit their new found agility. It's a fascinating year, but one which is also marked for most parents and children by the fact that at some point, your child will probably begin to go to school.

The turbulence of this new experience combined with a strong desire to fit in with classmates can sometimes cause your child to lock in their creativity as they adjust to the rules and expectations of life in school. Instead of happily playing with modelling dough or splashing paint around, for example, they will begin to observe others closely and perhaps copy them, to ensure they 'do it right'.

In some respects, this behaviour helps children to learn important social skills, such as how to form friendships and consideration for others feelings. But in terms of creativity, many children start to really lose their individuality. You can help by pointing out and praising other children who demonstrate individuality and by creating an environment where your child is positively encouraged to think for themselves.

Golden rules

PRAISE THE PROCESS, NOT THE RESULTS

At this age especially, your child craves adult approval, but giving approval which implies you are judging the products of their creative efforts can stifle their creativity. Focus your attention and praise on the process of solving problems or creating artwork rather than the end result. At this age, your child will begin to feel insecure about the fact that their horse doesn't look like the one in the book, maybe even telling you the picture is something else because they couldn't make it look the way they wanted it to.

You can help by shifting attention and asking your child about the colours they chose and the interesting effect they achieved by using their paintbrush to dab instead of stroke because it's something new for them.

NEVER TELL THEM OFF FOR ASKING QUESTIONS

It's not easy, because now that your child has a full and flowing vocabulary and an intense curiosity about the world, they will be asking all kinds of questions, many of which may be difficult or embarrassing. Be prepared for your child to loudly question the gender of passers-by, or to comment on their appearance. Of course, children need to learn to respect other people's feelings, but make sure that they are not disciplined for asking questions. Try to answer questions as calmly and honestly as you can, within reason. If your child is repeatedly asking you questions which you believe they know the answer to, ask them what they think the answer is.

SET UP CREATIVE UNSTRUCTURED PLAY

Rather than expecting your child to participate in strictly scheduled painting or craft sessions, try to set out materials and resources so they can access them when they want to. At this age, children are beginning to understand they can work through their feelings through fantasy or creative activities, so try to set up craft boxes or easels so they can choose the activity which best suits their mood.

BE SLOW TO HELP

Four-year-olds trying to learn how to make something new, or write their first letters, often feel a huge sense of frustration that they can't learn quickly enough. Offer some advice from the sidelines, or just gentle reassurance that their efforts will result in eventual success. Above all, resist the temptation to step in and help. At best, your child will angrily insist that he or she wants to do it on their own, and feels slightly undermined that you have no faith they can eventually succeed. At worst, they will give in and begin to expect you to help them.

MAKE SURE THEY FEEL SAFE

We all make sure our children are as safe as possible. There is a subtle difference, however, between your child being in a safe environment and feeling emotionally secure. At this age, children are beginning to worry and have nightmares. They are only really beginning to separate the world of fantasy from reality and they are often plagued by worries which adults would never imagine were bothering them. Many studies have supported psychoanalyst Dr John Bowlby's theory which sets out that caregivers who are accessible and responsive to their young child's needs help to form a sense of security, which means that child will be braver in exploring his world, more likely to ask questions and to find new and unusual solutions to problems.

In order to provide this secure attachment, simply listen to your child and calmly talk through any worries or anxieties they have. Try to help them rationalize their fears and to feel powerful enough to overcome them.

Insight
Remember, your child will follow your lead when facing new situations. If you show you are anxious and upset, they'll feel they have reason to be frightened.

CELEBRATE THEIR INDIVIDUALITY

Many children of this age will begin school during this year and so peer pressure becomes a strong influence. They'll also be told repeatedly to do what the teachers tell them to do. Of course, your child needs to behave appropriately at school, but it is important to encourage your child to think of individuality as a good thing. Read appropriate stories such as *Elmer: The Story of a Patchwork Elephant* by David McKee and praise unique things about your child and about other children. Make a point of praising independent thinking, too. When your child comes up with a really novel or imaginative idea, for example, admire their originality, even if the idea or solution they have come up with is totally impractical.

Here are some games and activities which will help to foster your child's creativity at this age. If your child isn't very interested in the activity you have set up, it is best not to force the issue, but rather to set out several different toys or materials so they can lead the play.

Remember: Children develop at different paces. For this reason, it's a good idea to look in the chapters before and after this one and to choose the activities and games which are most appropriate for your child.

Games, toys and activities to play with your child

THINGS TO MAKE WITH YOUR CHILD

Make a kite
Your child can handle more complex tasks now, but might need help. Use the traditional method below, or, for a stronger kite, kite enthusiast Roy Reed has developed a brilliant home-made design using refuse bags and bamboo stakes which you can find online at his website www.reeddesign.co.uk.

You will need:

▶ *some plastic shopping bags or strong paper*
▶ *some bamboo or dowling*
▶ *string*
▶ *scotch tape or insulation tape.*

Cut the sticks into two pieces – 90 centimetres and 102 centimetres long, then make a cross by marking a point 45 centimetres down the longer stick and placing the shorter stick across it at right angles. Tie the sticks together tightly with string.

Cut notches in the ends of the sticks and loop string around each notch so that it forms a tight kite-shaped frame around the edge of the sticks.

Lay the kite frame down on the plastic bags or paper and draw the shape onto it. Mark another outline, adding a three-centimetre margin and cut it out. Stick the paper or plastic to the frame, folding the plastic or paper over the edges of the frame and sticking it so it is pulled tightly across the frame.

Using one piece of string, tie a loop around the top of the kite, another loop of string around the intersection in the middle, and a third around the bottom of the kite.

Cut another piece of string 1.5 metres in length then tie that through the loop at the bottom of the kite. This will be the tail of the kite. Tie ten ribbons along it.

Finally tie one end of a long roll of string to the bottom loop, this is the string you'll hold when you fly the kite, so you might want to wrap the remaining spare string around a piece of card or kitchen roll holder so you can wind it back and forth easily. Then simply wait for a windy day when you and your child can try it out.

Make pairs cards
This is a good activity to encourage your child to develop new designs, and for helping them to use their memory.

Take three pieces of A4 card, fold the card into quarters and cut into even pieces, so you have 12 altogether. Then, taking two cards at a time, colour in two cards with the same simple design. For example, your child might choose red triangles and blue circles. When you have decorated all 12 cards, jumble them up and lay them face down on the floor. Then each player turns over two cards at a time. If you get a pair, you keep them and have another go. If you don't then you replace both cards, trying to remember what and where they were, and let the next player have ago. The winner is the person with the most pairs at the end of the game.

THINGS FOR CHILDREN WHO LOVE SCIENCE

The vase experiment

Get some photos or pictures and put them behind a large, round glass vase full of water – they'll be the wrong way round. Have fun looking at the back-to-front pictures and experimenting with other glass containers to see what effects they have on the images.

Stargazing

Set out some comfortable chairs or cushions by the window on a clear night and show your child the stars. Telescopes make this easier, especially in areas with lots of streetlights as they reflect more starlight. There are plenty of children's telescopes available, you can buy them from most major toy shops and special websites such as www.scopesnskies.com. Visit websites such as that of The Society for Popular Astronomy website, www.popastro.com, or the Young Stargazers pages and Jodrell Bank Centre for Astrophysics at www.jodrellbank.manchester.ac.uk for regular updates of when you are most likely to see things of particular interest, such as shooting stars and planets.

Insight

Light pollution can make it hard to see the night sky in towns and cities. Visit the National Trust website at www.nationaltrust.org.uk to find their recommendation for the seven best places around the country to look at the stars.

Make a volcano

You will need:

▶ *1 kg/2 lb flour*
▶ *½ kg/1 lb salt*
▶ *4 tbsp cooking oil*
▶ *food coolouring*
▶ *a baking tray*
▶ *a small plastic bottle*

- *washing-up liquid*
- *vinegar*
- *2 tbsp of baking soda.*

First make the outside part of the volcano. Mix the flour, salt and cooking oil, and gradually add water until you have a firm dough. Then, colour it with red and green food colouring until it is brown and mould it into shape around the plastic bottle in the baking tray. Do not cover the hole at the top.

Almost fill the bottle with warm water and red food colouring. Then add six drops of washing-up liquid, two tablespoons of baking soda and then slowly pour in the vinegar and watch your volcano erupt.

Make sugar crystals
You will need:

- *a clear glass jar*
- *rough string*
- *a pencil*
- *kitchen roll*
- *sugar*
- *food colouring if required.*

Cut a length of string which will hang near the bottom of the glass jar when it's tied around the middle of a pencil lying across the top of the jar.

Pour some boiling water into a mug and stir in a teaspoon at a time of sugar, stirring constantly until you start to see a small amount of sugar at the bottom which will not dissolve. This part of the experiment needs to be conducted by an adult and watched by the child for safety reasons.

Pour the sugar solution into the clear jar and add one or two drops of food colouring – if you want a coloured crystal. Balance the pencil with the string over the top of the jar, so the string hangs inside without touching any of the sides. Put a piece of kitchen roll, or a coffee filter over the top. After a few days, you should see a crystal beginning to grow. When your crystal is the desired size, keep it somewhere warm and dry.

Make a cardboard thunderclap

The aim of this activity is to make a loud noise! Using the cardboard and paper you create a structure that when flicked through the air, forces the air out of the paper in such a way that you get a very loud bang. It encourages your child to start thinking about the way sound works as well as being lots of fun.

You will need:

▶ *strong A4 cardboard*
▶ *brown paper*
▶ *scissors*
▶ *sticky tape.*

Cut a triangle out from the bottom of the A4 piece of cardboard, make it as tall as it is wide. Cut a triangle about 9 inches by 6 out from the brown paper. Place the 9-inch edge along the bottom of the card triangle and stick it down. Score and fold the paper and card down its length, with the sticky tape inside. Then fold the cardboard in half with the brown paper inside so it's like a mini paper aeroplane. Hold the cardboard with the point facing down and bring your arm down through the air quickly and you should hear a nice loud crack.

Balloon magic

Tell your child that you're going to show them how to do some magic tricks with balloons. Then blow up a few balloons and rub them on your jumper, or another soft fluffy surface, so they gather plenty of static. First show your child the magic hair trick, by lifting the balloon a few centimetres over their heads so that their hair stands on end. Then move on to the next trick, rub the balloon again to build up static, start the cold water tap and let them see how the balloon will bend the water towards itself.

THINGS TO DO WITH COMPUTERS

Do some online exploring

Your child will be very curious about their everyday environment, but also beginning to be curious about places they have read about in books or seen on the television. The Internet is a wonderful way for children to start learning more about the rest of the world, different people, cultures and animals.

Ask your child to choose an animal they are interested in and use an online atlas to discover all about the environment where it comes from. The National Geographic website has a good atlas for children at www.nationalgeographic.com/kids-world-atlas/index.html.

THINGS TO DO INDOORS

Guess who charades

This game encourages children to practise acting skills. Each player takes turns to think of a member of your family and to mime a silent impersonation of that person. For example, you might want to be looking for your glasses if your chosen person is always doing that, or mimic a sibling playing with a favourite toy.

Make a sponge garden

You will need:

▶ *a natural sponge (from a chemist)*
▶ *some birdseed*
▶ *a pot.*

Put about 1 centimetre of water in a pot, then put the sponge in and sprinkle it with seed. Place it somewhere warm and sunny. As long as you keep the water at the same level you should get some little seeds sprouting.

Write secret messages
Your child might not be able to write many letters yet, but they can draw secret pictures.

Ask your child to write a secret message or draw a secret picture on a piece of white card using a white candle or crayon. Then, using water-based paints, paint over the top to reveal the secret code.

Family-animal characters
Ask your child to think of a member of the family or a family friend, and to do an impression of the animal that most reminds them of that family member. You have to guess what animal it is and who the family member is.

Bear in mind that your child's perceptions of what different animals represent may be very different to yours.

THINGS TO DO OUTSIDE

Message in a balloon
Ask your child to think of a message to tie to the balloon. They might want to draw a picture, or write their name and the email address of a grown-up, or just a simple positive message to the person who finds it. Give your child a day or two to think about the message they want to send and to prepare it. Seal the finished message with clingfilm or some waterproof covering. Fill the balloon and tie the message securely to it, then all gather round to mark the moment that your child lets the balloon fly up into the air.

Insight
Do take steps to protect your child's identity when trying this activity. Never send their full name and/or address out into the wide world.

The garden sounds game

If your garden isn't quiet you can do this in a park, in some nearby woods or at the seaside. Go somewhere peaceful where your child feels safe, and, making sure they can hear and touch you all the time, wrap a piece of cloth over their eyes, or ask them to close their eyes. Then ask them to list all the sounds they can hear and to try to guess what each sound is. Take a notebook or tape recorder and when you get home, ask your child if they'd like to draw some of the things that made the sounds.

Shadow catching

On a sunny day, spend some time playing with shadows. Play shadow tag, where the idea is that you touch someone's shadow and they are 'It'. Then get some big pieces of paper and crayons and help your child to draw around different shadows.

Make a wormery

Making a wormery teaches children about nature and encourages them to think creatively to find ways to search for the worms to go inside it.

You will need:

▶ *a big clear plastic bottle*
▶ *scissors*
▶ *compost*
▶ *sand*
▶ *newspaper*
▶ *sand and leaf litter*
▶ *dark paper or cloth*
▶ *a rubber band.*

First go worm hunting with a pot of compost or earth to put any worms you find into while you prepare the wormery. Ask the children to help think up places you might find worms – under rocks or bushes. If you're having difficulty, pour a watering can onto some grass and stamp up and down as this brings worms to the surface. Collect five or six worms.

Cut the top off your plastic bottle and make little holes in the bottom. Then put a thin layer of moistened, shredded newspaper in the bottom, followed by a thin layer of sand. Then add a thick layer of compost or earth and put the worms into this. Then repeat the layers, finally putting a layer of leaf litter and possibly vegetable peelings or old teabags on the top. Finally cover the top of the bottle with the paper or cloth and secure with a rubber band. Store the wormery somewhere dark for a week or so, keeping the contents slightly damp. Watch how the worms move around and see if they like eating the vegetable peelings and teabags. Before two weeks is up, release them.

The pin in the map game
You'll need a car, a map and a sense of adventure for this game.

On a weekend or free day, get a map of the local area and ask your child to close their eyes and put the pin in the map. The idea is that you all go to that place, or as near as you reasonably can for a picnic. The task may prove impossible, but equally, you could end up discovering a beautiful spot by the river or a fabulous view.

The mud hole
On a sunny day, dig a little hole in your garden, cut a bin liner in half and line the hole with it, then fill the hole with some of the earth you removed and add a small amount of water. Your child can make mud pies and enjoy getting messy, but do supervise this activity constantly.

Play the tree detective game
This is a good game for learning about nature, but also for using problem-solving and detective skills.

Find some pictures of six or seven leaves from different common trees and go on a nature trail to see if you can find the trees which the leaves come from. See how many trees you can track down. If you don't have a book with pictures of leaves, you can find some at www.naturedetectives.org.uk.

THINGS TO DO WITH ARTS AND CRAFTS

Make rock monsters
You will need:

- ▶ *some interestingly shaped stones collected on a walk*
- ▶ *googly eyes (from a craft shop)*
- ▶ *glue*
- ▶ *paint.*

Making sure your rocks are clean and flat, stick on their googly eyes, then paint their faces. You might like to hide them around the garden with your child as a surprise for visitors.

Painting with marbles
You will need:

- ▶ *some marbles*
- ▶ *paper*
- ▶ *2 trays with edges*
- ▶ *paint.*

Pour some paint into the first tray, and roll the marbles around it. Then place your paper into the clean tray, add the marbles and move the tray around to make marble paintings. Repeat with lots of different colours to make pretty pictures.

THINGS TO DO WITH MUSIC

Make a bells and ribbons dance
Tie some bells to your child's wrists and ankles and give them a long stretch of ribbon, lots of space and play some music. Encourage them to play with the movement of the ribbon and hear the bells as they move their arms and legs.

Paint a song
Play some music your child enjoys listening to. Then ask them to pick one song that they would like to paint. Keep playing the music

in the background, and don't give too much direction. If your child asks for help, ask what things the song makes them think about, or if they can imagine the song playing in the scene of a story.

> **Insight**
> Painting a song, some food, or a texture is a great way to open up new thought processes in your mind too – give it a try.

THINGS TO DO WITH SPORTS

Balloon volleyball
Balloons are good for all kinds of creative games, but this is a good game for encouraging your child to be physically creative and to promote hand-eye coordination.

Blow up a big balloon and then bat it to each other across the room or garden using your hands or feet. The game is that the balloon is never allowed to touch the floor, and you both have to work together to see how long you can keep it up in the air.

THINGS TO DO WITH BOOKS

Tell a what-happened-next story
This game isn't just good for helping your child to dream up stories, but also for helping to build their empathy skills.

Using a timer, set to about 30 seconds, take turns telling the story. You start, then every time the buzzer goes off, the next person has to continue the story. On the fifth go, the person has to finish the story. The 30-second limit will result in your children having to think of narrative off the top of their head, which encourages them to tap into their intuitive imagination.

Start a joke book
Children of this age love telling jokes. Start up a book for them, writing down some of their jokes, so they can make up their own special joke book. Try to make up some knock knock jokes using their names, and encourage them to think of new ones.

Share picture stories

Using old magazines or books your child has not yet read, look for pictures which show characters demonstrating different emotions and activities; the more ambiguous the pictures the better. Then show the pictures you've chosen to your child and explain you are all going to make up a different story about the pictures. Encourage your child to go first, and suggest ideas if required.

THINGS TO DO WITH FOOD

Make multicoloured lollies

Choose fruit juices that are of interesting colours and flavours, such as blackcurrant, mango, apple and even cranberry. Then pour the different flavours into lolly moulds (available at supermarkets or kitchen shops) or ice trays before leaving them in the freezer overnight.

Make a toast collage

Toast a piece of bread on one side. Then cut some ham, cheese and tomatoes into different shapes, then ask your child to make a picture out of them on the untoasted side. Then toast the sandwich under the grill and enjoy a very creative lunch.

10 THINGS TO REMEMBER

1 *Praise your child's efforts rather than judging the results. Children catch on quickly to false praise and this way you encourage persistence and will always have some genuine praise to offer.*

2 *Encourage your child to ask questions about things others take for granted.*

3 *Expect tantrums as they try to get things 'right' and feel frustrated, and remind them there is sometimes more than one right way to do things.*

4 *Don't dismiss or lie about emerging fears, but help your child to rationalize and overcome them.*

5 *Now is a great time to try basic science experiments such as growing crystals or seeing whether things float or sink.*

6 *Your child will want to fit in socially with their friends more and more now. It's good to be different, but remember it's not always easy!*

7 *Don't be too much of a perfectionist in front of your child.*

8 *Take time to appreciate the amazing creativity of your child right now. As Picasso once said: 'It took me four years to paint like Raphael, but a lifetime to paint like a child'.*

9 *Watch out for emotions and feelings your child is expressing through creative play which they don't yet have the vocabulary to tell you about.*

10 *Sometimes your child will be at their most creative when they are behaving badly. But being creative is not an excuse to disrespect the feelings and property of others.*

10

Five to six years

In this chapter you will learn:
- *how encouraging creativity can help your child to develop at this age*
- *the golden rules for encouraging creativity at this age*
- *activities and games which will enhance their natural curiosity and imagination.*

At five years old, your child is probably already sharing complex thoughts and stories with you. Psychologists have found that many five-year-olds have already learned the subtle, creative arts of flattery and manipulation.

In some ways, your child's imagination has never been more vivid. Most five-year-olds still love imaginary play and creative activities, and their rapidly growing knowledge and understanding of the world means they have a vast array of means to express their creativity, and lots of material to help them to form new ideas and to input into creative projects. However, your child is also now beginning to tell fantasy from reality, and prefers playing with other children rather than by him or herself.

It's around about now that your child needs you more than ever to help explain when fantasy is good, and when it's not appropriate; when it is acceptable to question rules, and when they must be followed. Children at this age need to learn the subtle art of understanding when it is good to be different and individual, and when rule breaking can threaten safety and the feelings and well-being of others.

As their worlds begin to become more and more complex, five-year-olds also need you, their family, to provide a sense of stability and emotional security.

> **Insight**
> One way to make sure your child feels emotionally safe is to make sure you are getting enough rest yourself, so you feel less stressed and calmer.

As your child develops and learns at an incredible pace, you may well be reaching the stage where they can help you to learn and broaden your own ideas and horizons just as much as you can teach them.

Golden rules

DON'T OVER INTELLECTUALIZE YOUR CHILD

Your child is probably already speaking in a very grown-up way, thanks to their new social skills. This is a time where you have to perform a very delicate balancing act. You have to respect your child, and talk to them in a manner that's not patronizing or dismissive, but also remember that they are still very young, and that although they can put on a good show, there are many things which are simply too complicated for them to understand.

Claire, mum to Callum, six, and Joe, five

CASE STUDY

'I've found the trick is to talk to them using the same language and tone you use for other adults, but to carefully edit the content of what you say so everything is straightforward and clear. I've found that if I'm being a bit too simple and patronizing, they'll quickly pick up on it, but if they don't understand something, they're less likely to admit it straight away.'

KEEP A GOOD ROUTINE

There might seem nothing creative or imaginative in sticking to the same routine, but it's vital for children of this age to have sound structure in their lives so they can feel a sense of security and reassurance which will encourage them to be more free in creative play. Try to have meals at the same time, and plan weekly activities at roughly the same time. Although the occasional adventure is fun, for the main part, your child's day-to-day life needs to centre around familiar places, people and activities.

Insight

In our busy world, trying to eat at the table is a good thing to fit into the daily routine, as whether they admit it or not, children love knowing there will be time in every day that they get to sit down and talk to you.

ONLY GIVE GENUINE PRAISE

Children of this age are often already able to distinguish between fake and genuine praise. Automatic or over-enthusiastic praise undermines the value of your approval, and also it dents the confidence of your child. It's instinctive, of course, to tell your child that the painting they've just handed to you is wonderful, but if they've just dashed off the sixth identical painting in a row with no special extra effort, thank them, without adding any extra comment, or ask an interested question about specific details of the picture without casting judgement.

AVOID GENDER STEREOTYPING

Children of this age become particularly aware of the differences between boys and girls and often play separately. Choose toys carefully and try to avoid falling into stereotypes at home. Allow your child to observe his mother doing some DIY or his father hanging the clothes out to dry. Buy your daughter toy cars and your son a cleaning or tea set and suggest ways they might bring those into their play.

HAVE LOTS OF ONE-TO-ONE TIME

Often children of this age can begin to feel jealous of younger siblings who still get to spend a lot more time with their parents or carers. Even if your child has no younger siblings, it can be testing for them to spend all day at school with people outside their family group. Make a special effort this year to pencil in lots of one-to-one time, even if you're just bringing them along shopping or sitting quietly reading stories together.

CONCENTRATE ON SPECIAL STRENGTHS

Because your child is spending so much time with other children, and also because their memory is expanding at this age, they're more likely to start comparing themselves and their abilities with other children. This can make them feel a lot more insecure. They might decide they're no good at painting or running races and be tempted to give up altogether. You can help to build your child's confidence by focussing on the areas where they have natural talent. But it's also crucial to make them aware that assets such as cleverness, sports abilities and creativity can be improved with effort and perseverance.

stories which show that persistence can win the day, and you don't have to be the biggest or loudest to win the day.

ASK FOR DETAILS ABOUT MAKE-BELIEVE GAMES

Your child will still have a rich fantasy life and love playing make believe. Ask interested questions about their play without casting judgement over their fantasy world.

Games, toys and activities to play with your five-year-old

Here are some games and activities which will help to unlock the creative potential of your youngster.

Remember: All children develop at different paces, so don't worry if your child isn't ready for some of these activities. Choose the things they're ready for and check back through the previous chapters to find a range of other games and activities that might be suitable for your child.

THINGS TO MAKE WITH YOUR CHILD

Make an ideas box
Paint an old box or container with bright colours, then ask your child to think of four or five things you'd like to do together another day. Every time your child has an idea of something they'd like to do, put it into the ideas box. Then, next time your child tells you they are bored, you can get the box out.

Insight
This activity also encourages your child to be more resourceful and proactive about planning their play.

Set up a role-play area
In your child's bedroom or in a playroom or corner of a room where they play a lot, set up an area for role play. For example,

you could use a cardboard box that you decorate differently
every so often to become a house or a pirate ship or a rocket.
Change the role-play area when your child becomes interested
in something new, after reading a book or watching something
on TV or talking about it with friends. Add dressing-up clothes,
books and other appropriate toys to encourage the play further.

THINGS TO DO ON THE COMPUTER

Send some e-cards
Help your child to develop keyboard and mouse skills, which
will become increasingly important to them, and get them to
do something thoughtful and creative for someone else by
helping them to sit down and send e-cards. Websites such as
www.uptoten.com and kids.yahoo.com/ecards have free e-cards
which children of this age can add simple personal touches to with
the mouse and then you can help them to type out their name and
a simple message.

THINGS TO DO INSIDE

Set up a wacky race
Using plastic containers, kitchen roll holders, empty boxes, bits
of old packaging and household items such as bowls and bits of
string, set up a big obstacle course for toy cars around the living
room. Kitchen roll holders can be tunnels, you can make bridges
out of boxes and mini mountains out of bowls. Let your
child come up with some ideas themselves for the race course.
Then take turns to race the cars around the track.

20 questions
You each think of a celebrity or someone you all know well and
pretend that you are that person. Then the other person has
20 questions to guess who that person is. The rules are that the
questions must be closed questions, therefore resulting in simple
yes or no answers, with no elaboration. If you get a yes answer

you get to ask another question, if you get a no answer it's the other person's turn to ask. The first one to guess who the person is pretending to be is the winner. If there is just two of you playing the person guessing simply tries to guess the person using 20 questions or less.

Find an answer together
When your child asks you an interesting question, or gets set a challenge for homework, make a project out of finding different ways to look for the answer together. For example, you could suggest you go to the library, where you can look in some books, and then go on the computer. You might be able to think of people you could ask, for example, a vet or a nurse you know. Let your child lead the way in working out where the best places are to look for the answers. Remember the point is not so much about getting the answer quickly, as enjoying the journey to find it.

Make a masking tape maze
Visit one of the many maze generators you can find online. There's a good one at www.glassgiant.com where you can tell it how tricky you want the maze to be. Print off the outline and then copy it onto your living room floor or garden with some carefully laid masking tape. Put some treasure in the middle and see how long it takes your child to find their way to it.

Two facts and a fib
Each person takes turns to say two true things and one lie. For example, you could say: 'Today I went shopping, yesterday I bought a doughnut and ate it secretly in the café, and tomorrow I've booked myself into a belly dancing class.' This game helps in developing empathy and humour, as well as helping you all to learn more about each other.

The good shoe hunt
Get six or seven pairs of shoes and hide one of each pair around the house. Set a timer for 10 minutes and see if your child can find all the missing shoes before the time is up.

THINGS TO DO OUTSIDE

Make leaf creatures
Gather interesting leaves and flowers and without any glue or paper, start making little creatures, for example, you could use little flowers for eyes, small leaves for ears, stems for arms or legs.

Make a bird feeder
You will need:

- *plastic bottles*
- *scissors*
- *clean yoghurt pots or milk cartons*
- *string*
- *birdseed.*

Cut a hole in the side of your plastic bottle to allow a fairly free flow of seeds. Don't make the hole so huge that they all come pouring out at once though. Make a few tiny holes at the bottom of the bottle to let rainwater drain out. Pierce a hole in the lid of the bottle and tie it firmly with strong string to a tree or from a washing line – ideally away from a spot where cats can easily hide and jump out at it! Put the birdseed into the feeder and keep watch for your new visitors. Keep the birdseed clean and refill the feeder regularly.

Top tip
For more ideas on how to keep the birds happy in your garden visit the Royal Society for the Protection of Birds website and see their make-and-do section, www.rspb.org.uk.

THINGS TO DO WHEN YOU'RE OUT AND ABOUT

Have a number hunt
When you go on a shopping trip or an outing, give each member of the family a number and see how many times they can spot that number while you're out. This is a good game for car journeys too and will encourage your child to think of new places such as doors,

car number plates and road signs where they might spot their number.

THINGS INVOLVING TECHNOLOGY AND SCIENCE

Make a video
Suggest to your child that you make a video together, of a holiday, or about a new pet, or another topic which they are really interested in at the moment. They might want to have a go holding the camera or spend time talking to you about the topic in front of it.

Magic tricks with water
One idea is the cork in the water game. Fill a glass almost to the top with water and ask your child to get the cork in the centre. No matter how carefully they do it, the surface tension will drag it to the side. Then you slowly add water until the water is slightly bulging over the top of the glass and put the cork in. Now the surface tension works to keep your cork right in the middle.

Another trick is the magic egg trick. Fill a glass three-quarters full with water and put in an egg. It will sink, then add salt, gradually stirring it in and the egg should rise as the salt makes the water more dense.

THINGS TO DO WITH ARTS AND CRAFTS

Make your own fridge magnets
You will need:

- *½ kg/1 lb baking soda*
- *1 cup cornstarch*
- *8 fl oz water*
- *paint and paintbrushes*
- *magnet strips (from a craft shop or old fridge magnets)*
- *glue.*

Put the baking soda and cornstarch into a saucepan and gradually add the water, stirring until it's smooth. Cook over medium heat, stirring until the mixture is dough-like. Take out the mixture and let it cool so your child can knead and flatten it. Let your child use cookie cutters or plastic knives to cut out shapes. Leave the shapes to dry overnight. The next day paint and decorate the shapes, then glue the magnet strips to the back.

Make a rainbow
This activity is designed to help your child learn about mixing colours.

Draw out the shape of the rainbow together, and with your child, name all seven colours of the rainbow and label them. Then tell your child the game is to get all the different colours from four paints – red, blue, yellow and white. Stand back at this point and give the minimum amount of help until your child begins to get bored or frustrated. Let them play with the colours and practise mixing lots of different shades. It doesn't matter if they don't end up with a perfect rainbow, just that they enjoy the process of learning about colours.

Make your own tattoos
Using bought face paints or home-made ones (see Chapter 8) take turns to paint your own temporary tattoos on each other. You can draw and cut out your own stencils, or print them off from designs online. If you want to buy proper body art stencils, they cost from just 30 pence from websites such as www.glitterbodyart.co.uk, or you can just use ordinary craft stencils. Do make sure your child has no cuts or sensitive skin before you start painting.

THINGS TO DO WITH MUSIC

Go to a concert
Your child's attention span is much longer now they're five, so it's a good time to take them to a live music event. Research the event to ensure it is age appropriate and that it is not a sit down event but one where your child can move around and make some noise if they wish to. There are lots of options available. Smaller festivals such as the Cambridge Folk Festival are ideal for children

of all ages and have special musical workshops for young children. Websites such as that of The Prince's Foundation for Children and the Arts have listings of local music events for children, www.childrenandarts.org.uk. There are lots of classical music events just for children too; www.bachtrack.com has a list of all classical music events for children by region, and there are often fun sessions such as face painting, and storytelling with music at these events.

The mood music game

Play this game to encourage your child to think about their personal responses to music. Play ten different pieces of music in a row for your child and for each one ask them if they think it's happy, sad, angry, tired – how does the music make them feel. Reassure them there is no 'right' answer.

THINGS TO DO INVOLVING DRAMA

Go to a play

Around now is an age where your child might love a day out to watch a play especially for children. Theatrical companies such as Paradox Theatre and Quicksilver Theatre tour the whole country putting on shows and drama workshops especially for young children, and it's very likely that your local theatre will have some similar events especially designed to get younger children interested in drama. Check your local listings, or websites such as www.paradoxtheatre.co.uk or www.quicksilvertheatre.org or the Professional Theatre for young audiences website, www.ctctheatre.org.uk, where you can find plays that are suitable for specific ages. You can find other plays and drama events at The Prince's Foundation for Children and the Arts at www.childrenandarts.org.uk.

Put on a spoon puppet show

Your child will be able to perform little plays around about now, so putting on a puppet show is a fun way to get creative – making your own puppets and performing the show. If you need inspiration for a script for the puppet show, websites such as that of The Creativity Institute, www.creativityinstitute.com, have links to free comedy scripts as well as some tips on how to write a simple script for a puppet show.

You will need:

- *as many wooden spoons as you have characters*
- *a big cereal box*
- *A4 card*
- *scissors*
- *straws*
- *double-sided sticky tape or glue*
- *a felt-tip marker*
- *old material*
- *wool*
- *paint.*

THE STAGE

Cut away most of the front of the cereal box leaving a 1 inch margin around the edge. This is the 'front' of the stage. Then cut away the long edge of the box which is going to be the bottom of the stage, so the spoons can pop up and down onto the stage. Draw your background scenes on some A4 card and stick two straws to the edges so you can pop the right scenes up and down in the play. Next, paint the outside of the box, and stick some material for curtains to the edge.

Your stage is now ready.

THE PUPPETS

Glue on strips of wool and draw faces onto the back of the spoons for the puppets' faces, and cut out bits of cloth and stick them down for their clothes.

Have a few practice runs of your script without being on stage. Then, for the show, stick the cereal box stage onto a large piece of card with a hole cut out to allow the spoons to pop up and down in the stage area. Stick the box down onto the card with sticky tape, and prop the card over the edge of a table so the hole is visible over the edge of the table and secure the card which is on the table with sticky tape. Cover the table with a tablecloth to hide the card and the puppet masters underneath, and begin your show.

THINGS TO DO WITH SPORTS

Go roller skating/ice skating
As well as helping them to develop their physical skills in a creative way, skating is a good way for children to learn that sometimes a little care and patience is needed, but that with practice, they will get better. If you don't have an ice rink near you, fit them out with pads and helmet and go roller skating in the local park. Sometimes children can benefit from holding on to a chair, or some ice rinks provide bars for children to hold, until they begin to feel more confident standing up and moving forwards and keeping their balance. If you can, hold your child's hands and skate backwards as they move forwards to help them on their first attempts.

Set up a sports cupboard
Your child is just testing their physical strengths and abilities at the moment, and driving them towards one sport in particular might be a bit off-putting if they're not naturally drawn to it. A good way to help them try out different things in their own time is to make a sports box and fill it with lots of different things, such as different shapes and sizes of balls, badminton sets, hula hoops, mini golf sets, bats, goalposts – whatever sporty toys and games you happen to have. They can then access this whenever they want and play different sports as the mood takes them.

Trampoline memory game
If you don't have a trampoline, you might like to play a similar game in a swimming pool. The game is that the first person jumps on the trampoline and makes an interesting move, maybe sitting down and jumping back up. The second person does the first move, and then makes up a new move to go with it, maybe sitting down

then jumping up and spinning around. Each person taking the next turn has to do all the moves that went before and add a new one, until someone forgets one of the moves. The children will be having so much fun and concentrating so hard on remembering, they won't even realize they are being creative by making up the next move.

THINGS TO DO WITH BOOKS

Real life heroes
Your child's at an age now where they are beginning to tell fantasy from reality and to compare what they read in books with what they experience in the real world. No doubt they have their favourite superheroes of the moment, but see if you can find some real life examples of their superheroes, so they can begin to see that they too can achieve incredible things in their own lives with a little creativity and courage. For example, you might find a real life firefighter in the newspaper who's just like Fireman Sam, or an animal rescuer or wildlife conservationist who's like Diego, or an explorer like Dora.

Top tip
Try to find people who are real life examples of the fictional characters they particularly love and admire and show them photos, talk about what they do, and maybe go online so you can discover more about the person together.

Have a big word of the week
Suggest to your child that they nominate a special new word that they've learned each week. If you happen to spot an unusual word they don't know in a story, for example, you can pick that out to be your next word of the week. Write the word on some paper and pin it to the fridge or noticeboard. The game is that you have to try to slip it into the conversation as many times as you can before the week is up. Your child will get to learn how it's used in lots of different contexts and will keep an eye out for interesting and unusual words.

Read the picture
Reading is important to your child, but illustrations still play a huge part in their imagination and understanding of the world. Find a beautifully illustrated storybook, and ask your child to look at the first picture and tell you what they think the story might be about, who might be in it, and then ask them if by looking at the picture they can think of what might happen next in the story and how it might end.

THINGS TO DO WITH FOOD

Have a new food night
Children of this age are notoriously bad at trying new foods, so try to introduce a ritual into your week when all the family try something new. Take turns for each member of the family to suggest something.

Make apple pizzas
Breaking the rules and doing something a bit different is in the true spirit of unlocking your child's creativity. This recipe is the perfect example.

For the base:

- *225 g/8 oz self-raising flour*
- *50 g/1.75 oz butter or margarine*
- *1 egg*
- *4 fl oz milk.*

For the topping:

- *1 cooking apple*
- *1 tbsp butter*
- *60 g/2 oz sugar*
- *1 tbsp flour*
- *1 tsp cinnamon.*

The base: Rub the flour and butter together until they're like breadcrumbs. Beat in the egg and then gradually add enough milk to make a soft dough and knead lightly. Divide the dough into four pieces and pat into little circles. Place these on greased baking sheets. Cook at 200°C/gas mark 6 for 15 minutes or until golden brown.

The topping: Make this while the pizza cooks. Core, peel and slice the apple. Melt the butter in a pan and add the apples, sugar, flour and cinnamon. Simmer until the slices are golden brown and then remove from the heat to cool. When the base is brown, remove from the oven and allow to cool slightly before spreading the apples over the top. Serve when the apple has cooled slightly and is safe for the children.

10 THINGS TO REMEMBER

1 *Your five-year-old is probably getting very good at flattery and manipulation!*

2 *Your child is more able now to tell fantasy from reality, so be careful not to undermine their trust in you by underestimating their grasp of reality.*

3 *Your child's world is getting very complicated and uncertain, so they need stability and routine at home.*

4 *Don't over-intellectualize your child, especially if they are very clever. Your five-year-old might seem very grown up, but emotionally and socially, they are still very little.*

5 *Don't be biased in the toys you choose and watch carefully to see which toys your child chooses on play dates and at school – they may not be the toys you think they like the most.*

6 *Have one-to-one time every day.*

7 *Point out any special strengths your child displays.*

8 *Teach your child that some talents come with practice, including things such as being clever, or being friendly.*

9 *Encourage your child to think up their own games and activities if they complain they are bored.*

10 *Physical play can be very creative too, whether it's dancing, making shapes during trampoline jumps or making up new ball games.*

More things to do

In this chapter you will learn:
- *more ideas for activities and games suitable for all ages.*

Five fun recipes to cook

EGG BOATS

You will need:

▶ *eggs*
▶ *peppers.*

Boil some eggs, peel them and cut them in half. Cut coloured peppers into triangle shapes for the sails.

FRUIT CATERPILLARS

You will need:

▶ *soft fruits, or tinned fruit such as peaches, melon and pears*
▶ *an apple*
▶ *raisins*
▶ *thin straws.*

Chop up chunks of soft fruit, and help your child thread them onto the straws to make the body of the fruit caterpillars.

Then use a spoon to take two scoops of apple, a smaller one for the tail a bigger one for the head. Use two bits of straw for the antennae and raisins for the eyes.

HOME-MADE LEMONADE

You will need:

- ▶ *6 lemons*
- ▶ *2 litres of cold water*
- ▶ *225 g/8 oz sugar*
- ▶ *ice cubes.*

Cut the lemons in half and squeeze them into a large jug. Remove any seeds. Add the sugar then stir in the water. Add in some ice cubes.

GINGERBREAD HOUSES

Combine storytelling and baking by making these gingerbread treats before reading your children *Hansel and Gretel*.

You will need:

- ▶ *125 g/4 oz unsalted butter*
- ▶ *100 g/3.5 oz dark muscovado sugar*
- ▶ *4 tbsp golden syrup*
- ▶ *325 g/11.5 oz plain flour*
- ▶ *1 tsp bicarbonate of soda*
- ▶ *2 tsp ground ginger*
- ▶ *icing sugar*
- ▶ *flaked almonds*
- ▶ *sweets of your choice.*

Preheat the oven to 170°C, gas mark 3. Line baking trays with greaseproof paper.

Melt the butter, sugar and syrup in a medium saucepan, stirring occasionally, then remove from the heat. Sieve the flour, ginger and bicarbonate of soda into a bowl and stir in the melted ingredients to make a stiff dough. Turn out onto a lightly floured surface and roll to a thickness of about 5 millimetres.

Cut out a triangle for the roof, and a large rectangle for the front of the house and a smaller one for a chimney. Bake for 9 or 10 minutes until light golden brown. When cooled, make up some glace icing by adding water to the icing sugar until it forms a sticky consistency. Brush the icing over the triangle then place the flaked almonds on top to be the roof tiles. Then, using the icing to help secure the sweets, decorate your house with doors and windows. Then sprinkle with icing sugar for a finishing touch.

SNOWBALL MONSTERS

You will need:

- *125 g/4 oz white chocolate*
- *rice cereal*
- *sweets*
- *cupcake cases.*

Melt the chocolate in a large bowl and mix in the rice cereal until you have a firm mixture. Then form balls with the mixture and put them into the cupcake cases and decorate with sweets to make eyes, fangs, and wiggle worm sweets for hair, too. Leave to cool and set.

Five fun ball games to play

PAN CATCH

Mark a spot where the player will stand and set out some different sized pots and pans from the cupboard, at increasing distances away, around the living room. See what the furthest pan is that your child can throw the ball into.

FOOTBALL SKITTLES

Set up some skittles or plastic bottles and play bowling, with players using their feet to send the ball towards your skittles.

A BOUNCE BALL OBSTACLE COURSE

Using toys, plant pots and hula hoops, set up an obstacle course for your child to weave around while constantly bouncing a ball and see how quickly they can make it round.

CATCH AND THROW

A twist on catch is for you and your child to have two balls and both throw and catch them to each other at the same time. You'll have to do some problem solving to work out the best way to do it.

THE BOUNCE EXPERIMENT

Gather as many balls as you can in your back garden, and using a hard floor surface near a wall, get your child to bounce them and mark on the wall in chalk how high each one bounces, to compare them.

Five things to do on long car journeys

THE ANIMAL NAME GAME

One person starts off by saying the name of an animal and everyone has to go around in turns saying a different animal. If someone repeats one, they are out and become a referee. The winner is the person left at the end who hasn't repeated any animals. This can be done with other objects too, for example, colours or places.

PLAY CAR SNOOKER

Each child has to shout out or tick off when they see the colour of a car, using snooker colours. Start with red, then yellow, green, brown, blue, pink (it's better to use purple if you don't want a long period of silence at this point) with the first person to get all the way to black as the winner.

THE QUESTION GAME

One person in the car starts with a question, for example, 'Where are we going?' and the second person has to continue the conversation with another question, and everyone takes turns. The first person to say something that isn't a question is the loser and the sillier the questions the better.

TALKING BOOKS

There are a huge range of children's stories available in CD or cassette format for child entertainment which will stimulate their imagination and yet be as effective as a car DVD. Visit the Talking Book Shop, www.talkingbooks.co.uk, to see a range of good children's stories.

ALPHABET PICTURES

Give your child some crayons and paper, and with your help they have to shout out the name of something beginning with each letter of the alphabet they see and draw it. You'll probably need to step in with some inventive ways around Y Yellow van, or X Crossroads sign...!

Five fun things to do in the park

HAVE A ROLL RACE

Set up a start and finish line and have a race with your child to see who can roll sideways the fastest to the end.

LET'S PRETEND SLIDING GAME

Play a game where your child has to come down the slide pretending to be different things, for example, a monkey, a tree, daddy...

THE MARTIAN GAME

Pretend to be an alien visiting earth for the first time and ask your child to explain to you what all the things are, and what they are for.

TWIG PICTURES

Gather up as many twigs as you can and make pictures out of them on the grass.

ANIMAL BINGO

Make a card of common animals you might see in the park, for example dogs, squirrels, ducks, and get your child to tick them off as they see them.

Five fun craft activities

MAKING PAPER FLOWERS

You will need:

▶ *pipe cleaners or florists wire*
▶ *coloured tissue paper*
▶ *glue*
▶ *sticky tape*
▶ *safety scissors.*

Cut several flower shapes or circles from the tissue paper, and cut small holes in the centre. Then cut some small five-pence-piece-sized circles from the tissue paper. Twist one end of a piece of wire and thread several flower shapes on via the other end and secure just underneath the twisted top of the wire by wrapping sticky tape around the underside of the tissue and the wire. Then dab the twisted wire and inner edges of the topside of the tissue paper with glue and stick on a coloured circle.

SPLATTER T-SHIRTS

You will need:

- *1 or 2 plain white T-shirts*
- *brightly coloured fabric paints (available from craft shops)*
- *paintbrushes*
- *newspaper.*

Put two or three colours of fabric paint into plastic cups, and put a paintbrush in each pot. Lay out lots of newspaper and the white T-shirt on top of it. Explain to your child they have to flick the paint onto the T-shirt without the brush ever touching the T-shirt. Leave to dry.

MAKE AN AQUARIUM

You will need:

- *a clear plastic pot or bottle with a wide opening (blue tinted plastic containers work well)*
- *green tissue paper*
- *pebbles and/or shells/sand*
- *cotton*
- *card*
- *paints*
- *glitter*
- *sticky tape.*

Put scrunched up green tissue paper and your pebbles, shells and sand into the bottom of the plastic container. Draw and colour in fish shapes and wavy lines of seaweed with paint and glitter and cut them out. Cut a circle of card about 1 centimetre wider than the opening of the bottle or pot. Cut out different lengths of cotton, and secure the one end to the top of the fish or seaweed with sticky tape and the other to one side of the card circle. Carefully push your fish and seaweed into the pot or bottle and place the card over the top of the opening. Stick the card down around the edge of the opening with stick tape.

MAKE MASKS

You will need:

- ▶ *a tape measure*
- ▶ *coloured card*
- ▶ *a stretch of elastic (available from the sewing section in supermarkets or in specialist shops)*
- ▶ *safety scissors*
- ▶ *glitter or whatever else you might like to use to decorate your mask.*

Measure the width of your child's forehead, the space between their eyes and the circumference of their head. Then mark on a coloured piece of card where your child's eyes need to be and help them cut out the rough shape of their mask so the mask covers their face and rests on their nose. Cut out the eye holes and pierce two small holes at the side of the mask for the elastic to go through. Then decorate the mask with feathers, glitter, paints, or whatever else your child might choose that you have to hand. When it's dry, cut a piece of elastic slightly shorter than the width you measured and tie the elastic through each ready-made hole, tying a knot in the ends and sticking down with sticky tape to secure.

MAKE A CUP GAME

You will need:

- ▶ *a paper cup*
- ▶ *a piece of string three times the length of the cup*
- ▶ *a plastic bottle top*

- ▸ *sticky tape*
- ▸ *paints to decorate.*

First paint and decorate your cup any way your child chooses. Pierce a small hole in the bottom of the paper cup, thread one end of the string through the top of the cup and stick it down securely underneath the cup. Pierce another hole in the plastic bottle top and thread the other end of the string through that, securing it by tying a knot in the end and sticking it down. The game is to hold the cup and try to get the bottle top on the end of the string into the cup.

Five fun musical activities

HAVE A FUNNY DANCE COMPETITION

See who can make everyone laugh the most with the funniest dance moves.

PLAY THE MUSICAL WORD GAME

Play pieces of music and ask your child to think of a word that they think of when they hear each one.

MAKE A DRUM

You will need:

- ▸ *a strip of strong but flexible card*
- ▸ *greaseproof paper*
- ▸ *sticky tape*
- ▸ *an elastic band.*

Cut a strip of card about 4 centimetres wide and form it into a circle, securing with sticky tape. Cut a circle, about 4 centimetres wider in diameter than the card circle, from the greaseproof paper, place it over the card circle so it is taut and secure it with the elastic band. Stick the band down with sticky tape to hold it in place. You can add sleigh bells to the edge of the card to make a tambourine.

MAKE WEATHER MUSIC

Gather as many musical percussion instruments as you can in a box and with your child try to make sounds that best suit different types of weather. For example, maracas could be rain, drums could be thunder, bells could be a breeze.

NAME THAT TUNE

Play a game where you sing just a few words of a favourite nursery rhyme or song and your child has to guess what the song is.

Five fun things to do at Christmas

MAKE HANDPRINT AND FOOTPRINT REINDEERS

You will need:

- ▶ *white card*
- ▶ *brown, red and yellow paint*
- ▶ *googly eyes*
- ▶ *glue*
- ▶ *newspaper.*

Put down lots of newspaper and some brown and yellow paint in wide flat trays. Dip your child's foot in the brown paint and get them to do one very careful footprint in the middle of the card. Then put one hand in the yellow paint, and assuming the toes are at the top of the reindeer's head, do two careful handprints for antlers. Paint a red nose at the end and stick on google eyes halfway down your footprint and you have a reindeer.

MAKE CHOCOLATE STAR DECORATIONS

You will need:

- ▶ *225 g/8 oz of sugar*
- ▶ *125 g/4.5 oz butter*
- ▶ *1 tsp vanilla essence*
- ▶ *1 egg*
- ▶ *225 g/8 oz self-raising flour*
- ▶ *dark cooking chocolate*
- ▶ *coloured ribbon.*

Place in a mixing bowl the sugar, butter and vanilla essence and cream together. Then add one egg, mix and then add the flour. Mix into a soft dough, then roll out and cut into star shapes. Cut out small holes in the top to hang ribbons through. Bake at 190°C for 15 to 20 minutes.

When cool, melt four chunks or 25 grams (1 ounce) of dark chocolate in a microwave or over a low heat in a saucepan. Wait until the chocolate is cool enough, but still soft for your child to help you. Then, using the round part of a spoon, drizzle chocolate in zigzags over the stars. Finally, thread the ribbons through to make charming tree decorations.

MAKE A SANTA CATCHER

Help your child set a Santa trap, by sprinkling icing sugar around the fireplace, so you can see if he might leave footprints in the night.

MAKE YOUR OWN WRAPPING PAPER

Using brown paper, use prints (or make them from potatoes, see Chapter 6) and stamp Christmas-themed designs such as trees, stars or holly to make your own designer wrapping paper.

HAVE YOUR OWN CHRISTMAS CONCERT

Take it in turns to each play, sing or dance a Christmas carol for each other one evening. Make a production of it and serve with popcorn or mince pies.

Five fun things to do at Easter

MAKE EGG PEOPLE

You will need:

▶ *eggs*
▶ *paint*
▶ *wool*
▶ *glue*
▶ *googly eyes.*

Pierce one small hole in the top of an egg and a larger one in the bottom. Then, using a straw, blow the egg white and yoke into a bowl and leave the egg to dry. Then, using wool for hair, paint your own egg men, women, animals or monsters and stick on googly eyes where appropriate. Your child will have to be very careful here and very delicate in their decoration so to not break the eggs.

MAKE AN EASTER GARDEN

You will need:

▶ *a cereal box*
▶ *moss*
▶ *stones*
▶ *twigs*
▶ *paint*
▶ *flowers.*

Cut the front off a cereal box, and using moss for the base, add stones, flowers and twigs for trees to make your own Easter garden. You can also paint the back of the box so that there is a nice pretty background to your garden.

HAVE AN EGG AND SPOON RACE

Boil some eggs and paint each person's a different colour. Then mark out a race track and the game is that the person has to carry their egg on their spoon from the start to the finish line without touching their egg with their hands. The first person to cross the finish line is the winner.

MAKE A GIANT CHOCOLATE NEST

You will need:

▶ *a 17-centimetre/7-inch cake tin*
▶ *greaseproof paper*
▶ *bran cereal*
▶ *250 g/9 oz cooking chocolate*
▶ *chocolate eggs.*

Line the base and edges of the cake tin with greaseproof paper. Melt the cooking chocolate in the microwave or over a low heat in a saucepan, then mix in the bran cereal. Add this to the cake tin and then add coloured eggs to the centre for all the family to share for a big Easter treat.

MAKE EASTER CHICKS

You will need:

▶ *cotton wool balls*
▶ *pipe cleaners*
▶ *card*
▶ *orange and yellow paint*

- *googly eyes*
- *glue*.

Paint a cotton wool ball yellow, paint the pipe cleaners and some card orange. When dry, cut out small triangles from card for the beaks and stick onto the cotton wool along with the googly eyes. Twist pipe cleaners into feet and glue on.

Conclusion

Many parents will begin reading this book with wonderful intentions to spend hours engaged in fun, creative play with their children, encouraging and praising them in just the right way. We all have visions of being perfect parents, going that extra mile to make sure our children are happy and engaged, doing arts and crafts, enjoying physical sports and activities, and never allowing them to feel bored or sitting them in front of the TV while we do our chores. Real life is very different of course.

But you don't have to be a perfect parent to free your child's creative potential. Perhaps the most beautiful aspect of children's creativity is that above all, it simply requires freedom. Children's creativity flourishes best in a safe, calm environment where you have simply left out plenty of appropriate toys and materials for them to play with.

And as you focus on your child's creative potential, take time to unlock your own. Spending time enjoying creative activities yourself, even if you don't think you're that good at them, is a valuable demonstration for your child that creative activities are enjoyable and worthwhile long past the time that your child leaves their preschool years.

And when you introduce novelty and imagination into your day-to-day life with your children, you'll add real magic and wonder to their early memories.

Perhaps the greatest lessons we can learn about creativity, however, are those we can learn from our children. While as carers, we can play a huge role in nurturing their creativity, it's a given fact that preschoolers are often far more intuitively imaginative, curious and open-minded than adults. Watch the way they question the world and dream, and we can learn to unlock our own creativity, even as we help to develop and sustain theirs.

Taking it further

Resources

FINDING CREATIVE TOYS

The Creativity Institute is an online toy shop specializing in toys and resources which will help to stimulate your child's imagination and problem-solving skills. Their website also has several interesting articles about different aspects of childhood creativity. Visit www.creativityinstitute.com.

Brightminds at www.brightminds.co.uk is another good website which helps you to find toys based on your child's age and interests. The Early Learning Centre also stocks a wide range of toys and activities and clearly labels those which help children of different ages to develop creative thinking and skills.

TOY LIBRARIES

Toy libraries offer valuable resources to families, children and carers by providing a wide range of carefully selected toys to borrow for nominal fees and often for free. This enables parents and carers to provide children with a wide range of resources to stimulate creative play without having to spend a great deal of money. To find out more about the services which Toy Libraries offer, and to find out information on your local Toy Library, contact the National Association of Toy and Leisure Libraries. Tel: 020 7428 2288 or visit www.natll.org.uk.

CHILDREN'S SCRAPSTORES

This is a national charity which collects unused materials from businesses, including everything from boxes and buttons to paper and plastic tubs. These unwanted goods are then distributed to scrapstores around the country so that families and educational institutions can make use of them in children's play and creative activities. The visits to the scrapstores in themselves are wonderful experiences for children, and suggested donations for trolleys of 'scrap' are around £12.50. This is therefore a very cost-effective way to gather an intriguing range of useful and inspiring materials. Visit www.childrensscrapstore.co.uk or call 0117 908 5644 to find out more, including your local children's scrapstore.

CREATIVE EVENTS AND WORKSHOPS

There are a rich variety of opportunities for children to experience cultural and creative events organized specifically to inspire a love of creativity. The Prince's Foundation for Children and the Arts has over 300 events running throughout the UK, including everything from musical workshops to storytelling festivals and dramatic productions. You can find more details of local events at their website www.childrenandarts.org.uk. Tests are also available at www.expertrating.com/childrens-creativity-test.asp.

CREATIVITY TESTING

You can order formal tests of your child's creativity via the Scholastic Testing Service, which offers the Figural part of the Torrance Test of Creative Thinking which is the most widely used test. Alternatively, you can find an educational psychologist who carries out creativity testing in your area at www.educational-psychologist.co.uk or through the British Psychological Society at www.bps.org.uk. Visit the American Psychological Association, www.apa.org, to find an expert in the US.

GIFTED CHILDREN

If your child seems to learn far more quickly than others in their age group and is highly creative, it's possible that your child may be gifted. This is a double-edged sword, because while it is wonderful that your child is talented, gifted children can often feel frustrated and can develop behavioural issues, and parents often find they have no one to share their experiences with. The screening process to determine giftedness is quite complex, but you can find out more and get support through the National Association for Gifted Children at www.nagcbritain.org.uk, Tel: 0845 4500295. In the US, visit the website of the National Association of Gifted Children www.nagc.org.

Recommended reading

These books may help to unleash your own imagination and creativity so you can help your child:

Bevan, R. & Wright, T. *Unleash Your Creativity: Secrets of Creative Genius* (Infinite Ideas Company, 2005).

For more ideas:

Bolton, V. *365 Things to Make and Do* (Parragon, 2003).

Milne, L. *Fun Factory: Games and toys from household rubbish* (Reader's Digest, 1995).

Simon, S. *101 Amusing Ways to Develop Your Child's Thinking Skills and Creativity* (RGA, 1989).

To find out how creativity is encouraged in early years education:

Bruce, T. *Cultivating Creativity in Babies, Toddlers and Young Children* (Hodder Education, 2004).

Craft, A. *Creativity and Early Years Education: A Lifewide Foundation* (Continuum, 2002).

Mayesky, M. *How to Foster Creativity in all Children* (Thomson, 2003).

For dads in particular:

Caplin, S. and Rose, S. *Dad Stuff* (Simon & Schuster, 2005).

To help your child express creativity through artwork:

Cassou, M. and Tarcher, J. P. *Kids Play: Igniting Children's Creativity* (Penguin, 2004).

Micklethwaite, L. *A Child's Book of Play in Art* (Dorling Kindersley, 1996).

To learn more about what creativity is:

Csikszentmihalyi, M. *Creativity* (HarperCollins, 1996).

Csikszentmihalyi, M. *Flow: The Classic Work on How to Achieve Happiness* (Rider & Co, 2002).

For older children:

Csikszentmihalyi, M., Rathunde, K., Whalen, S. *Talented Teenagers: The Roots of Success and Failure* (Cambridge University Press, 1997).

Duffy, B. *Supporting Creativity and Imagination in the Early Years* (Open University Press, 1998).

To discover how parental praise influences creativity:

Dweck, C. S. *Mindset: The New Psychology of Success* (Ballantine, 2006).

Ellison, S. and Gray, J. *365 Days of Creative Play* (Sourcebooks, 1995).

For games and activities to help your newborn to 12-month-old baby to develop new skills:

Stoppard, M. *Baby's First Skills: Help your Baby Learn Through Creative Play* (Dorling Kindersley, 2005).

Index